PUZZLE PACK
for
Sounder

based on the book by
William Armstrong

Written by
Mary B. Collins

© 2005 Teacher's Pet Publications
All Rights Reserved

The materials in this packet are copyrighted
by Teacher's Pet Publications, Inc.

These pages may be duplicated by the purchaser
for use in the purchaser's own classroom.

Copying any of these materials and distributing them
for any other purpose is a violation of the copyright laws.

© 2005 Teacher's Pet Publications, Inc.
www.tpet.com

INTRODUCTION
If you already own the LitPlan for this title, this Puzzle Pack will refresh your Unit Resource Materials and Vocabulary Resource Materials sections plus give you additional materials you can substitute into the tests. If you do not already have a complete LitPlan, these pages will give you some supplemental materials to use with your own plan. There are two main groups of materials: one set for unit words (such as characters' names, symbols, places, etc.) and one set for vocabulary words associated with the book.

WORD LIST
There is a word list for both the unit words and the vocabulary words. These lists show you which words are being used in the materials and the clues or definitions being used for those words. You may want to give students a word list with clues/definitions to help them, or you may want students to only have a word list (without clues/definitions) if you want them to work a little harder. Both are available for duplication. The word lists can also be your "calling key" for the bingo games.

FILL IN THE BLANK AND MATCHING
There are 4 each of the fill in the blank and matching worksheets for both the unit and vocabulary words. These pages can be used either as extra worksheets for students or as objective parts of a unit test. They can be done individually if students need extra help or as a whole class activity to review the material covered.

MAGIC SQUARES
The magic squares not only reinforce the material covered but also work on reasoning and math skills. Many teachers have told us that their students really enjoy doing these!

WORD SEARCH PUZZLES
The word search words go in all directions, as indicated on your answer keys. Two of the word search puzzles have the clues listed rather than the words. This makes the puzzle a little more difficult, but it reinforces the material better. Two word search puzzles have words only for students who find the clue puzzles too difficult.

CROSSWORD PUZZLES
Both unit and vocabulary word sections have 4 crossword puzzles.

BINGO CARDS
There are 32 individual bingo cards for the unit words and 32 individual bingo cards for the vocabulary words. You can use your word list as a "call list," calling the words at random and marking them off of your list as you go, or you could use the flash cards by cutting them apart and drawing the words at random from a hat (or box or whatever). To make a better review, you might ask for the definition and spelling of each word as you call it out–or you could call out the definitions and have students tell you the words they need to look for on the puzzle.

JUGGLE LETTERS
The vocabulary juggle letter game is intended to help students learn the spellings of the words. One sheet has the definitions listed on it as an extra help for students who need it or to reinforce the definitions if you choose to do so.

FLASH CARDS
We've included a set of vocabulary flash cards you can duplicate, cut, and fold for your students. Some teachers make a few sets for general use by the class; others make a set for each student. Some teachers duplicate them for each student and have the students cut & fold their own. You can cut out just the words and put them in a hat, have each student pick out one word and write the definition and a sentence for that word. Students then swap words and papers, with the next student adding a sentence of his own under the last one. You can have students swap as many times as you like. Each time the student will read the sentences written prior to his own and then add a sentence. You can cut out the words and definitions separately and play "I Have; Who Has?" Each student in the room draws a word and definition. The first student says, "I have (the name of the word). Who has the definition?" The student with the definition reads it then says, "I have (the name of the vocabulary word she has). Who has the definition?" The round continues until all words and definitions have been given.

Sounder Unit Word List

No.	Word	Clue/Definition
1.	BARK	Upon his return, Sounder would not ____; he would only whine
2.	BIBLE	Book with stories the boy liked
3.	BOX	They put the cake in one
4.	CAKE	Mother baked one for Father
5.	CALF	Bottom part of the leg
6.	CHILDREN	The boy's mother told him not to leave them alone
7.	CHRISTMAS	Holiday season
8.	COONDOG	Sounder was one of these
9.	CRIPPLED	What Sounder and Father became
10.	CURTAINS	Eyes watched from behind these
11.	DIE	Stop living
12.	EAR	The boy found Sounder's
13.	EARTH	Dirt; our planet
14.	FATHER	He was sent to a labor camp
15.	HAM	The stolen kind of meat
16.	HAND	The boy's hurt appendage
17.	HUMMED	What Mother did when she worried
18.	HUNT	Look for animals to shoot
19.	JOURNEY	A trip
20.	KERNEL	Nut meat
21.	LANTERN	Lamp; usually has oil fuel
22.	LAW	Police enforce it
23.	MAGAZINES	The boy found these to read
24.	MOTHER	She returned the stolen meat
25.	MUSH	What the family ate when they did not have meat
26.	NICKS	Small cuts and gouges
27.	PILLOWCASE	This was washed every week
28.	PORCH	Sounder crawled under it
29.	PREACHER	The father would send word with him
30.	READ	The boy wanted to do this
31.	REAL	Actual; true; not imagined
32.	RED	The ____ faced man at the jail
33.	RUIN	The red-faced man ____ed the cake
34.	SAUSAGES	Mother returned the pork____
35.	SCHOOL	Place one goes to learn
36.	SHARECROPPERS	The family's occupation
37.	SHERIFF	County law enforcer
38.	SHOTGUN	Sounder was shot by one
39.	SOUNDER	The dog's name
40.	SOWBELLY	Item on Mother's shopping list
41.	STEAL	To take something that isn't yours
42.	TEACHER	Instructor
43.	TO	The father went ____ jail
44.	TWO	Sounder was away for ____ months
45.	WALNUT	The mother picked these kernels
46.	WOODPILE	Where wood is kept

Sounder Fill In the Blank 1

_____

_____

_____

_____

_____

_____

_____

_____

_____

_____

_____

_____

_____

_____

_____

_____

_____

_____

_____

_____

1. Police enforce it
2. He was sent to a labor camp
3. She returned the stolen meat
4. The ____ faced man at the jail
5. The boy's mother told him not to leave them alone
6. What Sounder and Father became
7. A trip
8. Book with stories the boy liked
9. The boy wanted to do this
10. Where wood is kept
11. Mother returned the pork____
12. The red-faced man ____ed the cake
13. Sounder was away for ____ months
14. Item on Mother's shopping list
15. Instructor
16. The boy found these to read
17. County law enforcer
18. To take something that isn't yours
19. The father would send word with him
20. Mother baked one for Father

Sounder Fill In The Blank 1 Answer Key

LAW	1. Police enforce it
FATHER	2. He was sent to a labor camp
MOTHER	3. She returned the stolen meat
RED	4. The ____ faced man at the jail
CHILDREN	5. The boy's mother told him not to leave them alone
CRIPPLED	6. What Sounder and Father became
JOURNEY	7. A trip
BIBLE	8. Book with stories the boy liked
READ	9. The boy wanted to do this
WOODPILE	10. Where wood is kept
SAUSAGES	11. Mother returned the pork____
RUIN	12. The red-faced man ____ed the cake
TWO	13. Sounder was away for ____ months
SOWBELLY	14. Item on Mother's shopping list
TEACHER	15. Instructor
MAGAZINES	16. The boy found these to read
SHERIFF	17. County law enforcer
STEAL	18. To take something that isn't yours
PREACHER	19. The father would send word with him
CAKE	20. Mother baked one for Father

Sounder Fill In The Blank 2

_____

_____

_____

_____

_____

_____

_____

_____

_____

_____

_____

_____

_____

_____

_____

_____

_____

_____

_____

_____

1. Police enforce it

2. What Sounder and Father became

3. Where wood is kept

4. To take something that isn't yours

5. The mother picked these kernels

6. Lamp; usually has oil fuel

7. Item on Mother's shopping list

8. Actual; true; not imagined

9. Book with stories the boy liked

10. What the family ate when they did not have meat

11. Dirt; our planet

12. The boy wanted to do this

13. The red-faced man ____ed the cake

14. Upon his return, Sounder would not ____; he would only whine

15. The boy found these to read

16. Instructor

17. Eyes watched from behind these

18. The boy's hurt appendage

19. What Mother did when she worried

20. The father would send word with him

Sounder Fill In The Blank 2 Answer Key

LAW	1. Police enforce it
CRIPPLED	2. What Sounder and Father became
WOODPILE	3. Where wood is kept
STEAL	4. To take something that isn't yours
WALNUT	5. The mother picked these kernels
LANTERN	6. Lamp; usually has oil fuel
SOWBELLY	7. Item on Mother's shopping list
REAL	8. Actual; true; not imagined
BIBLE	9. Book with stories the boy liked
MUSH	10. What the family ate when they did not have meat
EARTH	11. Dirt; our planet
READ	12. The boy wanted to do this
RUIN	13. The red-faced man ____ed the cake
BARK	14. Upon his return, Sounder would not ____; he would only whine
MAGAZINES	15. The boy found these to read
TEACHER	16. Instructor
CURTAINS	17. Eyes watched from behind these
HAND	18. The boy's hurt appendage
HUMMED	19. What Mother did when she worried
PREACHER	20. The father would send word with him

Sounder Fill In The Blank 3

_____

1. A trip
2. The family's occupation
3. She returned the stolen meat
4. Where wood is kept
5. They put the cake in one
6. The stolen kind of meat
7. Bottom part of the leg
8. The dog's name
9. Dirt; our planet
10. The boy's mother told him not to leave them alone
11. The _____ faced man at the jail
12. Place one goes to learn
13. Instructor
14. Mother returned the pork_____
15. Upon his return, Sounder would not _____; he would only whine
16. Lamp; usually has oil fuel
17. This was washed every week
18. Holiday season
19. Sounder was one of these
20. What the family ate when they did not have meat

Sounder Fill In The Blank 3 Answer Key

JOURNEY	1. A trip
SHARECROPPERS	2. The family's occupation
MOTHER	3. She returned the stolen meat
WOODPILE	4. Where wood is kept
BOX	5. They put the cake in one
HAM	6. The stolen kind of meat
CALF	7. Bottom part of the leg
SOUNDER	8. The dog's name
EARTH	9. Dirt; our planet
CHILDREN	10. The boy's mother told him not to leave them alone
RED	11. The ____ faced man at the jail
SCHOOL	12. Place one goes to learn
TEACHER	13. Instructor
SAUSAGES	14. Mother returned the pork____
BARK	15. Upon his return, Sounder would not ____; he would only whine
LANTERN	16. Lamp; usually has oil fuel
PILLOWCASE	17. This was washed every week
CHRISTMAS	18. Holiday season
COONDOG	19. Sounder was one of these
MUSH	20. What the family ate when they did not have meat

Sounder Fill In The Blank 4

1. Book with stories the boy liked
2. Sounder crawled under it
3. Actual; true; not imagined
4. Item on Mother's shopping list
5. The stolen kind of meat
6. The father would send word with him
7. They put the cake in one
8. What the family ate when they did not have meat
9. The boy's hurt appendage
10. Holiday season
11. A trip
12. The boy wanted to do this
13. This was washed every week
14. Place one goes to learn
15. What Sounder and Father became
16. The red-faced man ____ed the cake
17. Instructor
18. Upon his return, Sounder would not ____; he would only whine
19. The mother picked these kernels
20. Bottom part of the leg

Sounder Fill In The Blank 4 Answer Key

BIBLE	1. Book with stories the boy liked
PORCH	2. Sounder crawled under it
REAL	3. Actual; true; not imagined
SOWBELLY	4. Item on Mother's shopping list
HAM	5. The stolen kind of meat
PREACHER	6. The father would send word with him
BOX	7. They put the cake in one
MUSH	8. What the family ate when they did not have meat
HAND	9. The boy's hurt appendage
CHRISTMAS	10. Holiday season
JOURNEY	11. A trip
READ	12. The boy wanted to do this
PILLOWCASE	13. This was washed every week
SCHOOL	14. Place one goes to learn
CRIPPLED	15. What Sounder and Father became
RUIN	16. The red-faced man ____ed the cake
TEACHER	17. Instructor
BARK	18. Upon his return, Sounder would not ____; he would only whine
WALNUT	19. The mother picked these kernels
CALF	20. Bottom part of the leg

Sounder Matching 1

___ 1. HAM A. The boy's mother told him not to leave them alone
___ 2. KERNEL B. Police enforce it
___ 3. RUIN C. Mother returned the pork____
___ 4. EARTH D. Look for animals to shoot
___ 5. BOX E. Sounder was shot by one
___ 6. HUMMED F. What the family ate when they did not have meat
___ 7. SOWBELLY G. Actual; true; not imagined
___ 8. CHILDREN H. Nut meat
___ 9. JOURNEY I. The father would send word with him
___ 10. PORCH J. County law enforcer
___ 11. READ K. The boy's hurt appendage
___ 12. REAL L. The red-faced man ____ed the cake
___ 13. TEACHER M. Instructor
___ 14. SAUSAGES N. Eyes watched from behind these
___ 15. PILLOWCASE O. This was washed every week
___ 16. HUNT P. What Mother did when she worried
___ 17. STEAL Q. They put the cake in one
___ 18. SCHOOL R. Item on Mother's shopping list
___ 19. HAND S. Dirt; our planet
___ 20. MUSH T. The stolen kind of meat
___ 21. PREACHER U. Place one goes to learn
___ 22. CURTAINS V. The boy wanted to do this
___ 23. LAW W. A trip
___ 24. SHOTGUN X. To take something that isn't yours
___ 25. SHERIFF Y. Sounder crawled under it

Sounder Matching 1 Answer Key

T - 1. HAM	A. The boy's mother told him not to leave them alone
H - 2. KERNEL	B. Police enforce it
L - 3. RUIN	C. Mother returned the pork____
S - 4. EARTH	D. Look for animals to shoot
Q - 5. BOX	E. Sounder was shot by one
P - 6. HUMMED	F. What the family ate when they did not have meat
R - 7. SOWBELLY	G. Actual; true; not imagined
A - 8. CHILDREN	H. Nut meat
W - 9. JOURNEY	I. The father would send word with him
Y - 10. PORCH	J. County law enforcer
V - 11. READ	K. The boy's hurt appendage
G - 12. REAL	L. The red-faced man ____ed the cake
M - 13. TEACHER	M. Instructor
C - 14. SAUSAGES	N. Eyes watched from behind these
O - 15. PILLOWCASE	O. This was washed every week
D - 16. HUNT	P. What Mother did when she worried
X - 17. STEAL	Q. They put the cake in one
U - 18. SCHOOL	R. Item on Mother's shopping list
K - 19. HAND	S. Dirt; our planet
F - 20. MUSH	T. The stolen kind of meat
I - 21. PREACHER	U. Place one goes to learn
N - 22. CURTAINS	V. The boy wanted to do this
B - 23. LAW	W. A trip
E - 24. SHOTGUN	X. To take something that isn't yours
J - 25. SHERIFF	Y. Sounder crawled under it

Sounder Matching 2

___ 1. SOUNDER
___ 2. TWO
___ 3. EARTH
___ 4. TEACHER
___ 5. HUMMED
___ 6. TO
___ 7. DIE
___ 8. BARK
___ 9. HAM
___ 10. LAW
___ 11. BOX
___ 12. KERNEL
___ 13. SHARECROPPERS
___ 14. CALF
___ 15. READ
___ 16. WALNUT
___ 17. JOURNEY
___ 18. WOODPILE
___ 19. SOWBELLY
___ 20. RUIN
___ 21. MOTHER
___ 22. MUSH
___ 23. SHOTGUN
___ 24. NICKS
___ 25. PORCH

A. Where wood is kept
B. Upon his return, Sounder would not ____; he would only whine
C. Instructor
D. Stop living
E. Dirt; our planet
F. They put the cake in one
G. The boy wanted to do this
H. Bottom part of the leg
I. The red-faced man ____ed the cake
J. The family's occupation
K. A trip
L. Sounder crawled under it
M. Police enforce it
N. The stolen kind of meat
O. Small cuts and gouges
P. The dog's name
Q. Sounder was shot by one
R. Nut meat
S. The father went ____ jail
T. She returned the stolen meat
U. Item on Mother's shopping list
V. Sounder was away for ____ months
W. What the family ate when they did not have meat
X. The mother picked these kernels
Y. What Mother did when she worried

Sounder Matching 2 Answer Key

P - 1. SOUNDER	A. Where wood is kept
V - 2. TWO	B. Upon his return, Sounder would not ____; he would only whine
E - 3. EARTH	C. Instructor
C - 4. TEACHER	D. Stop living
Y - 5. HUMMED	E. Dirt; our planet
S - 6. TO	F. They put the cake in one
D - 7. DIE	G. The boy wanted to do this
B - 8. BARK	H. Bottom part of the leg
N - 9. HAM	I. The red-faced man ____ed the cake
M -10. LAW	J. The family's occupation
F -11. BOX	K. A trip
R -12. KERNEL	L. Sounder crawled under it
J -13. SHARECROPPERS	M. Police enforce it
H -14. CALF	N. The stolen kind of meat
G -15. READ	O. Small cuts and gouges
X -16. WALNUT	P. The dog's name
K -17. JOURNEY	Q. Sounder was shot by one
A -18. WOODPILE	R. Nut meat
U -19. SOWBELLY	S. The father went ____ jail
I -20. RUIN	T. She returned the stolen meat
T -21. MOTHER	U. Item on Mother's shopping list
W -22. MUSH	V. Sounder was away for ____ months
Q -23. SHOTGUN	W. What the family ate when they did not have meat
O -24. NICKS	X. The mother picked these kernels
L -25. PORCH	Y. What Mother did when she worried

Sounder Matching 3

___ 1. DIE
___ 2. MAGAZINES
___ 3. CAKE
___ 4. JOURNEY
___ 5. MOTHER
___ 6. TEACHER
___ 7. SHARECROPPERS
___ 8. HUNT
___ 9. TWO
___10. KERNEL
___11. FATHER
___12. LANTERN
___13. SOWBELLY
___14. CHILDREN
___15. EARTH
___16. WOODPILE
___17. NICKS
___18. CHRISTMAS
___19. CRIPPLED
___20. PREACHER
___21. RUIN
___22. COONDOG
___23. BOX
___24. BARK
___25. BIBLE

A. He was sent to a labor camp
B. A trip
C. Upon his return, Sounder would not ____; he would only whine
D. Dirt; our planet
E. Lamp; usually has oil fuel
F. Look for animals to shoot
G. Mother baked one for Father
H. They put the cake in one
I. Stop living
J. She returned the stolen meat
K. The father would send word with him
L. Nut meat
M. The boy found these to read
N. Item on Mother's shopping list
O. Sounder was away for ____ months
P. What Sounder and Father became
Q. The boy's mother told him not to leave them alone
R. The family's occupation
S. Book with stories the boy liked
T. Holiday season
U. Instructor
V. Where wood is kept
W. Small cuts and gouges
X. Sounder was one of these
Y. The red-faced man ____ed the cake

Sounder Matching 3 Answer Key

I - 1. DIE
M - 2. MAGAZINES
G - 3. CAKE
B - 4. JOURNEY
J - 5. MOTHER
U - 6. TEACHER
R - 7. SHARECROPPERS
F - 8. HUNT
O - 9. TWO
L - 10. KERNEL
A - 11. FATHER
E - 12. LANTERN
N - 13. SOWBELLY
Q - 14. CHILDREN
D - 15. EARTH
V - 16. WOODPILE
W - 17. NICKS
T - 18. CHRISTMAS
P - 19. CRIPPLED
K - 20. PREACHER
Y - 21. RUIN
X - 22. COONDOG
H - 23. BOX
C - 24. BARK
S - 25. BIBLE

A. He was sent to a labor camp
B. A trip
C. Upon his return, Sounder would not ____; he would only whine
D. Dirt; our planet
E. Lamp; usually has oil fuel
F. Look for animals to shoot
G. Mother baked one for Father
H. They put the cake in one
I. Stop living
J. She returned the stolen meat
K. The father would send word with him
L. Nut meat
M. The boy found these to read
N. Item on Mother's shopping list
O. Sounder was away for ____ months
P. What Sounder and Father became
Q. The boy's mother told him not to leave them alone
R. The family's occupation
S. Book with stories the boy liked
T. Holiday season
U. Instructor
V. Where wood is kept
W. Small cuts and gouges
X. Sounder was one of these
Y. The red-faced man ____ed the cake

Sounder Matching 4

___ 1. CHRISTMAS A. The boy wanted to do this
___ 2. WOODPILE B. The family's occupation
___ 3. PORCH C. The stolen kind of meat
___ 4. BOX D. What the family ate when they did not have meat
___ 5. JOURNEY E. A trip
___ 6. MUSH F. Lamp; usually has oil fuel
___ 7. NICKS G. Sounder crawled under it
___ 8. SAUSAGES H. Actual; true; not imagined
___ 9. HUNT I. Sounder was shot by one
___ 10. SHARECROPPERS J. To take something that isn't yours
___ 11. RED K. The boy's hurt appendage
___ 12. HAND L. Police enforce it
___ 13. LANTERN M. The dog's name
___ 14. SOUNDER N. Small cuts and gouges
___ 15. REAL O. Where wood is kept
___ 16. CAKE P. Mother baked one for Father
___ 17. CRIPPLED Q. Sounder was one of these
___ 18. READ R. The ____ faced man at the jail
___ 19. EAR S. Holiday season
___ 20. LAW T. Look for animals to shoot
___ 21. BIBLE U. They put the cake in one
___ 22. HAM V. Mother returned the pork____
___ 23. STEAL W. The boy found Sounder's
___ 24. SHOTGUN X. Book with stories the boy liked
___ 25. COONDOG Y. What Sounder and Father became

Sounder Matching 4 Answer Key

S - 1.	CHRISTMAS	A. The boy wanted to do this
O - 2.	WOODPILE	B. The family's occupation
G - 3.	PORCH	C. The stolen kind of meat
U - 4.	BOX	D. What the family ate when they did not have meat
E - 5.	JOURNEY	E. A trip
D - 6.	MUSH	F. Lamp; usually has oil fuel
N - 7.	NICKS	G. Sounder crawled under it
V - 8.	SAUSAGES	H. Actual; true; not imagined
T - 9.	HUNT	I. Sounder was shot by one
B - 10.	SHARECROPPERS	J. To take something that isn't yours
R - 11.	RED	K. The boy's hurt appendage
K - 12.	HAND	L. Police enforce it
F - 13.	LANTERN	M. The dog's name
M - 14.	SOUNDER	N. Small cuts and gouges
H - 15.	REAL	O. Where wood is kept
P - 16.	CAKE	P. Mother baked one for Father
Y - 17.	CRIPPLED	Q. Sounder was one of these
A - 18.	READ	R. The ____ faced man at the jail
W - 19.	EAR	S. Holiday season
L - 20.	LAW	T. Look for animals to shoot
X - 21.	BIBLE	U. They put the cake in one
C - 22.	HAM	V. Mother returned the pork____
J - 23.	STEAL	W. The boy found Sounder's
I - 24.	SHOTGUN	X. Book with stories the boy liked
Q - 25.	COONDOG	Y. What Sounder and Father became

Sounder Magic Sqares 1

Match the definition with the vocabulary word. Put your answers in the magic squares below. When your answers are correct, all columns and rows will add to the same number.

A. STEAL
B. CURTAINS
C. CALF
D. SOUNDER
E. RED
F. KERNEL
G. LAW
H. BIBLE
I. JOURNEY
J. SHOTGUN
K. SHERIFF
L. EAR
M. PORCH
N. SOWBELLY
O. HAND
P. BOX

1. Bottom part of the leg
2. Sounder was shot by one
3. Nut meat
4. The boy's hurt appendage
5. They put the cake in one
6. The ____ faced man at the jail
7. A trip
8. The dog's name
9. Sounder crawled under it
10. Book with stories the boy liked
11. The boy found Sounder's
12. To take something that isn't yours
13. Eyes watched from behind these
14. County law enforcer
15. Police enforce it
16. Item on Mother's shopping list

A=	B=	C=	D=
E=	F=	G=	H=
I=	J=	K=	L=
M=	N=	O=	P=

Sounder Magic Squares 1 Answer Key

Match the definition with the vocabulary word. Put your answers in the magic squares below. When your answers are correct, all columns and rows will add to the same number.

A. STEAL
B. CURTAINS
C. CALF
D. SOUNDER
E. RED
F. KERNEL
G. LAW
H. BIBLE
I. JOURNEY
J. SHOTGUN
K. SHERIFF
L. EAR
M. PORCH
N. SOWBELLY
O. HAND
P. BOX

1. Bottom part of the leg
2. Sounder was shot by one
3. Nut meat
4. The boy's hurt appendage
5. They put the cake in one
6. The ____ faced man at the jail
7. A trip
8. The dog's name
9. Sounder crawled under it
10. Book with stories the boy liked
11. The boy found Sounder's
12. To take something that isn't yours
13. Eyes watched from behind these
14. County law enforcer
15. Police enforce it
16. Item on Mother's shopping list

A=12	B=13	C=1	D=8
E=6	F=3	G=15	H=10
I=7	J=2	K=14	L=11
M=9	N=16	O=4	P=5

Sounder Magic Squares 2

Match the definition with the vocabulary word. Put your answers in the magic squares below. When your answers are correct, all columns and rows will add to the same number.

A. DIE
B. REAL
C. PORCH
D. SAUSAGES
E. SCHOOL
F. CAKE
G. BARK
H. NICKS
I. RED
J. FATHER
K. LANTERN
L. CALF
M. CHILDREN
N. HAM
O. EARTH
P. EAR

1. The stolen kind of meat
2. Upon his return, Sounder would not ____; he would only whine
3. Bottom part of the leg
4. Stop living
5. Lamp; usually has oil fuel
6. Actual; true; not imagined
7. The boy's mother told him not to leave them alone
8. Small cuts and gouges
9. Place one goes to learn
10. The boy found Sounder's
11. Sounder crawled under it
12. He was sent to a labor camp
13. Mother returned the pork ____
14. The ____ faced man at the jail
15. Mother baked one for Father
16. Dirt; our planet

A=	B=	C=	D=
E=	F=	G=	H=
I=	J=	K=	L=
M=	N=	O=	P=

Sounder Magic Squares 2 Answer Key

Match the definition with the vocabulary word. Put your answers in the magic squares below. When your answers are correct, all columns and rows will add to the same number.

A. DIE
B. REAL
C. PORCH
D. SAUSAGES
E. SCHOOL
F. CAKE
G. BARK
H. NICKS
I. RED
J. FATHER
K. LANTERN
L. CALF
M. CHILDREN
N. HAM
O. EARTH
P. EAR

1. The stolen kind of meat
2. Upon his return, Sounder would not ____; he would only whine
3. Bottom part of the leg
4. Stop living
5. Lamp; usually has oil fuel
6. Actual; true; not imagined
7. The boy's mother told him not to leave them alone
8. Small cuts and gouges
9. Place one goes to learn
10. The boy found Sounder's
11. Sounder crawled under it
12. He was sent to a labor camp
13. Mother returned the pork ____
14. The ____ faced man at the jail
15. Mother baked one for Father
16. Dirt; our planet

A=4	B=6	C=11	D=13
E=9	F=15	G=2	H=8
I=14	J=12	K=5	L=3
M=7	N=1	O=16	P=10

Sounder Magic Squares 3

Match the definition with the vocabulary word. Put your answers in the magic squares below. When your answers are correct, all columns and rows will add to the same number.

A. EARTH
B. SHERIFF
C. COONDOG
D. SHOTGUN
E. RUIN
F. CHILDREN
G. SOWBELLY
H. SCHOOL
I. KERNEL
J. TEACHER
K. CURTAINS
L. SOUNDER
M. READ
N. BIBLE
O. CALF
P. SHARECROPPERS

1. Dirt; our planet
2. Book with stories the boy liked
3. Instructor
4. The red-faced man ____ed the cake
5. Item on Mother's shopping list
6. The dog's name
7. The family's occupation
8. Sounder was one of these
9. Bottom part of the leg
10. Sounder was shot by one
11. Place one goes to learn
12. Eyes watched from behind these
13. Nut meat
14. The boy's mother told him not to leave them alone
15. County law enforcer
16. The boy wanted to do this

A=	B=	C=	D=
E=	F=	G=	H=
I=	J=	K=	L=
M=	N=	O=	P=

Sounder Magic Squares 3 Answer Key

Match the definition with the vocabulary word. Put your answers in the magic squares below. When your answers are correct, all columns and rows will add to the same number.

A. EARTH
B. SHERIFF
C. COONDOG
D. SHOTGUN
E. RUIN
F. CHILDREN
G. SOWBELLY
H. SCHOOL
I. KERNEL
J. TEACHER
K. CURTAINS
L. SOUNDER
M. READ
N. BIBLE
O. CALF
P. SHARECROPPERS

1. Dirt; our planet
2. Book with stories the boy liked
3. Instructor
4. The red-faced man ____ed the cake
5. Item on Mother's shopping list
6. The dog's name
7. The family's occupation
8. Sounder was one of these
9. Bottom part of the leg
10. Sounder was shot by one
11. Place one goes to learn
12. Eyes watched from behind these
13. Nut meat
14. The boy's mother told him not to leave them alone
15. County law enforcer
16. The boy wanted to do this

A=1	B=15	C=8	D=10
E=4	F=14	G=5	H=11
I=13	J=3	K=12	L=6
M=16	N=2	O=9	P=7

Sounder Magic Squares 4

Match the definition with the vocabulary word. Put your answers in the magic squares below. When your answers are correct, all columns and rows will add to the same number.

A. HAND
B. KERNEL
C. CURTAINS
D. CHILDREN
E. CRIPPLED
F. WOODPILE
G. HAM
H. SHARECROPPERS
I. HUNT
J. SAUSAGES
K. EARTH
L. REAL
M. WALNUT
N. READ
O. STEAL
P. TO

1. The mother picked these kernels
2. Where wood is kept
3. The family's occupation
4. To take something that isn't yours
5. Actual; true; not imagined
6. Eyes watched from behind these
7. The boy's hurt appendage
8. Mother returned the pork____
9. Dirt; our planet
10. The boy's mother told him not to leave them alone
11. Nut meat
12. Look for animals to shoot
13. The boy wanted to do this
14. What Sounder and Father became
15. The stolen kind of meat
16. The father went ____ jail

A=	B=	C=	D=
E=	F=	G=	H=
I=	J=	K=	L=
M=	N=	O=	P=

Sounder Magic Squares 4 Answer Key

Match the definition with the vocabulary word. Put your answers in the magic squares below. When your answers are correct, all columns and rows will add to the same number.

A. HAND
B. KERNEL
C. CURTAINS
D. CHILDREN
E. CRIPPLED
F. WOODPILE
G. HAM
H. SHARECROPPERS
I. HUNT
J. SAUSAGES
K. EARTH
L. REAL
M. WALNUT
N. READ
O. STEAL
P. TO

1. The mother picked these kernels
2. Where wood is kept
3. The family's occupation
4. To take something that isn't yours
5. Actual; true; not imagined
6. Eyes watched from behind these
7. The boy's hurt appendage
8. Mother returned the pork____
9. Dirt; our planet
10. The boy's mother told him not to leave them alone
11. Nut meat
12. Look for animals to shoot
13. The boy wanted to do this
14. What Sounder and Father became
15. The stolen kind of meat
16. The father went ____ jail

A=7	B=11	C=6	D=10
E=14	F=2	G=15	H=3
I=12	J=8	K=9	L=5
M=1	N=13	O=4	P=16

Sounder Word Search 1

```
L A W L K M U S H W B H R E D B R E S S
C A N Q P E C W H W A O U T G E I N A G
M Y N T H O R N J E K L X N H G I B Y R
D A O T O C R N I U R D N C T A F N L Z
D W G N E E V S E C C I A U T W U A L E
T R D A H R C T O L K E F R T G E H E Y
R O R T Z T N H G U R S U F T T C R B Y
G C A L F I D S I P N C C O S R R W W K
L F B C Q E N M A L C D H H O Y E P O Q
M H J Q M G C E K U D S E P O T A A S Y
L R C M J N R E S R S R Y R D O L P D F
D M U X L Z L R D R A A E W W T L P H X
W H T K Q I S G F V M X G N N E H X C W
S D R B P S K N W B T Z S E Q A C Q A L
Z A Y D J H F R Y X S W N V S C Z L K R
B Z O H R V V J R W I E A R T H A M E C
X O Y C Z B B J O U R N E Y W E A H D M
W Q N C P M R P Y Q H W C K L R T N L L
W W T R P I L L O W C A S E G O C G D B
Q F Z B C R I P P L E D Q N M P F R X N
```

A trip (7)
Actual; true; not imagined (4)
Book with stories the boy liked (5)
Bottom part of the leg (4)
County law enforcer (7)
Dirt; our planet (5)
Eyes watched from behind these (8)
He was sent to a labor camp (6)
Holiday season (9)
Instructor (7)
Item on Mother's shopping list (8)
Lamp; usually has oil fuel (7)
Look for animals to shoot (4)
Mother baked one for Father (4)
Mother returned the pork____ (8)
Nut meat (6)
Place one goes to learn (6)
Police enforce it (3)
She returned the stolen meat (6)
Small cuts and gouges (5)
Sounder crawled under it (5)
Sounder was away for ____ months (3)
Sounder was one of these (7)
Sounder was shot by one (7)
Stop living (3)
The ____ faced man at the jail (3)
The boy found Sounder's (3)
The boy found these to read (9)
The boy wanted to do this (4)
The boy's hurt appendage (4)
The boy's mother told him not to leave them alone (8)
The dog's name (7)
The father went ____ jail (2)
The father would send word with him (8)
The mother picked these kernels (6)
The red-faced man ____ed the cake (4)
The stolen kind of meat (3)
They put the cake in one (3)
This was washed every week (10)
To take something that isn't yours (5)
Upon his return, Sounder would not ____; he would only whine (4)
What Sounder and Father became (8)
What Mother did when she worried (6)
What the family ate when they did not have meat (4)
Where wood is kept (8)

Sounder Word Search 1 Answer Key

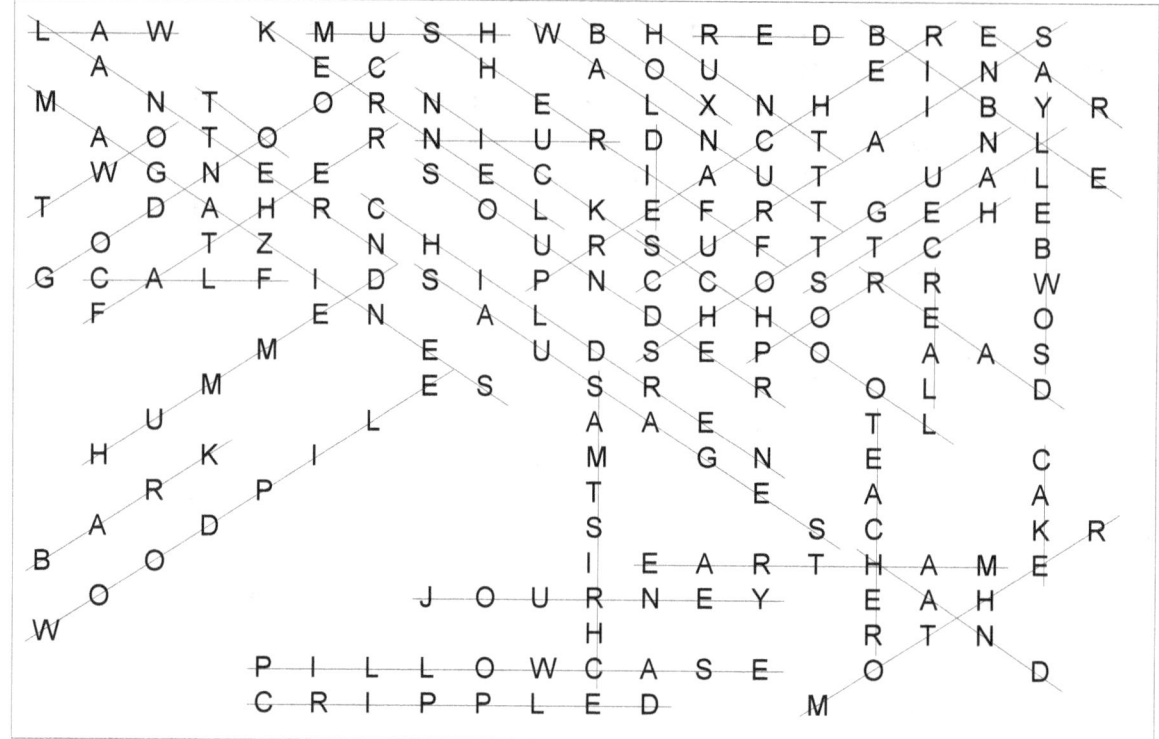

A trip (7)
Actual; true; not imagined (4)
Book with stories the boy liked (5)
Bottom part of the leg (4)
County law enforcer (7)
Dirt; our planet (5)
Eyes watched from behind these (8)
He was sent to a labor camp (6)
Holiday season (9)
Instructor (7)
Item on Mother's shopping list (8)
Lamp; usually has oil fuel (7)
Look for animals to shoot (4)
Mother baked one for Father (4)
Mother returned the pork____ (8)
Nut meat (6)
Place one goes to learn (6)
Police enforce it (3)
She returned the stolen meat (6)
Small cuts and gouges (5)
Sounder crawled under it (5)
Sounder was away for ____ months (3)
Sounder was one of these (7)
Sounder was shot by one (7)

Stop living (3)
The ____ faced man at the jail (3)
The boy found Sounder's (3)
The boy found these to read (9)
The boy wanted to do this (4)
The boy's hurt appendage (4)
The boy's mother told him not to leave them alone (8)
The dog's name (7)
The father went ____ jail (2)
The father would send word with him (8)
The mother picked these kernels (6)
The red-faced man ____ed the cake (4)
The stolen kind of meat (3)
They put the cake in one (3)
This was washed every week (10)
To take something that isn't yours (5)
Upon his return, Sounder would not ____; he would only whine (4)
What Sounder and Father became (8)
What Mother did when she worried (6)
What the family ate when they did not have meat (4)
Where wood is kept (8)

Sounder Word Search 2

```
M A G A Z I N E S M U S H S F X M S T O
A C G N P L I G B V F S H F F M N H U M
H A M K O K C M D A S M I E R I P O N Z
W L X N R S K P Q I R R L E A Z I T L B
V F I X C W S E L N E K H T V R L G A J
W U O H H L L E S H P C R U E Z L U W J
R B O B S B N J S X A U Y D N M O N X N
G O C L I R B M W E C T N N W T W P T B
L X M B E G N L R J O U R N E Y C T N N
P T Y K H N N P T W O B S C L B A C S Q
V C H R I S T M A S C R C T D G S R K S
S D G K L C H I L D R E N F E X E I B S
K O J K A L D V H F Q H P V A A H P J S
X M W R N N R Z A L K S P D R T L P J C
B Y L B T R N E N J A F C C E E H L D C
F H B B E L I P D O O W T E A C H E R F
R T P A R L G D F K V V R R L K M D R M
F X D S N Q L W D Y Y V T R G M E B B J
B M N R R F Y Y R G R H S A U S A G E S
J M G S C C O O N D O G K H M O T H E R
```

A trip (7)
Actual; true; not imagined (4)
Book with stories the boy liked (5)
Bottom part of the leg (4)
County law enforcer (7)
Dirt; our planet (5)
Eyes watched from behind these (8)
He was sent to a labor camp (6)
Holiday season (9)
Instructor (7)
Item on Mother's shopping list (8)
Lamp; usually has oil fuel (7)
Look for animals to shoot (4)
Mother baked one for Father (4)
Mother returned the pork____ (8)
Nut meat (6)
Place one goes to learn (6)
Police enforce it (3)
She returned the stolen meat (6)
Small cuts and gouges (5)
Sounder crawled under it (5)
Sounder was away for ____ months (3)
Sounder was one of these (7)
Sounder was shot by one (7)

Stop living (3)
The ____ faced man at the jail (3)
The boy found Sounder's (3)
The boy found these to read (9)
The boy wanted to do this (4)
The boy's hurt appendage (4)
The boy's mother told him not to leave them alone (8)
The dog's name (7)
The father went ____ jail (2)
The father would send word with him (8)
The mother picked these kernels (6)
The red-faced man ____ed the cake (4)
The stolen kind of meat (3)
They put the cake in one (3)
This was washed every week (10)
To take something that isn't yours (5)
Upon his return, Sounder would not ____; he would only whine (4)
What Sounder and Father became (8)
What Mother did when she worried (6)
What the family ate when they did not have meat (4)
Where wood is kept (8)

Sounder Word Search 2 Answer Key

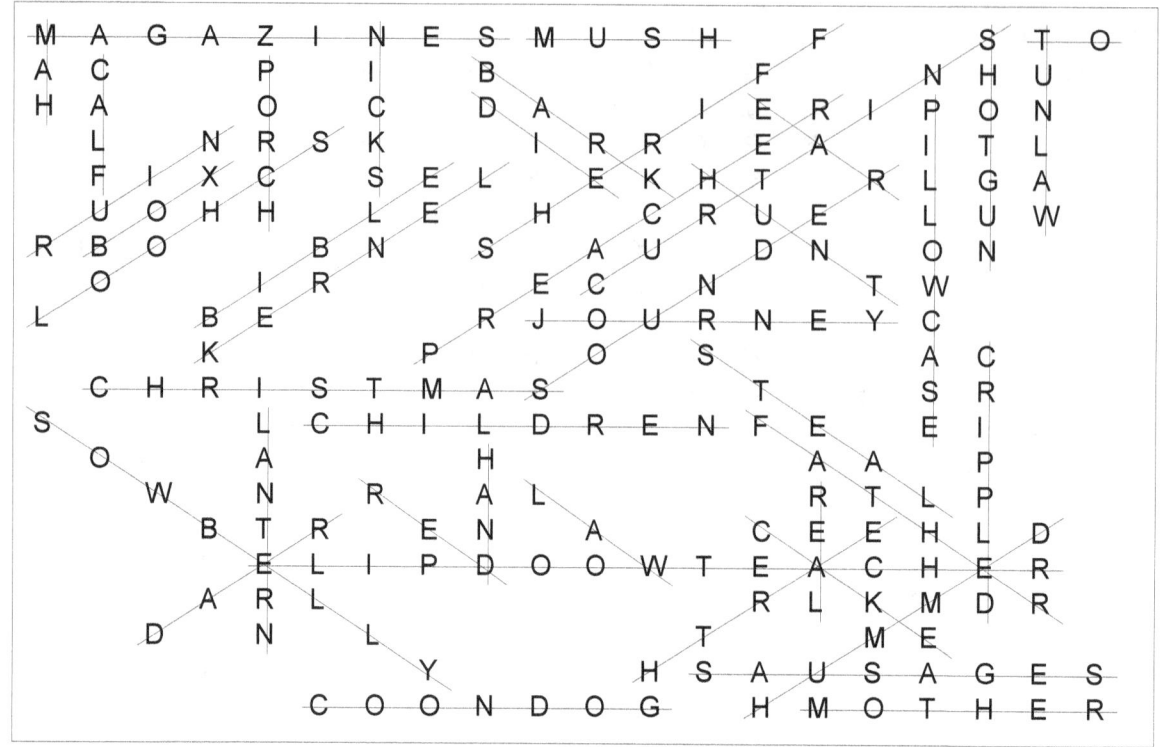

A trip (7)
Actual; true; not imagined (4)
Book with stories the boy liked (5)
Bottom part of the leg (4)
County law enforcer (7)
Dirt; our planet (5)
Eyes watched from behind these (8)
He was sent to a labor camp (6)
Holiday season (9)
Instructor (7)
Item on Mother's shopping list (8)
Lamp; usually has oil fuel (7)
Look for animals to shoot (4)
Mother baked one for Father (4)
Mother returned the pork____ (8)
Nut meat (6)
Place one goes to learn (6)
Police enforce it (3)
She returned the stolen meat (6)
Small cuts and gouges (5)
Sounder crawled under it (5)
Sounder was away for ____ months (3)
Sounder was one of these (7)
Sounder was shot by one (7)

Stop living (3)
The ____ faced man at the jail (3)
The boy found Sounder's (3)
The boy found these to read (9)
The boy wanted to do this (4)
The boy's hurt appendage (4)
The boy's mother told him not to leave them alone (8)
The dog's name (7)
The father went ____ jail (2)
The father would send word with him (8)
The mother picked these kernels (6)
The red-faced man ____ed the cake (4)
The stolen kind of meat (3)
They put the cake in one (3)
This was washed every week (10)
To take something that isn't yours (5)
Upon his return, Sounder would not ____; he would only whine (4)
What Sounder and Father became (8)
What Mother did when she worried (6)
What the family ate when they did not have meat (4)
Where wood is kept (8)

Sounder Word Search 3

```
C U R T A I N S L S S T N U H Y F E K S
S H F J X H O X A T H O E B P U S J E B
H Y R N P U K U N E W N W A I A M C R F
A R T I N F S J T A F E S B C B W M N X
R F P D S A K F E L C R H W E H L Y E Z
E K E R G T S X R H P D O D Z L E E L D
C R S E W H M M N F S L T T H Y L R F L
R S S H Z E H A P S L I G S V V D Y W B
O G Y C E R Y Y S I N H U D Z V F H D R
P Y G A X R B P P W R C N Q D X R L W Q
P P F E S N I C K S O C C L E D R L A K
E R W R X G D F H W Q O B N L X Q S L J
R L J P X P Y E F A J O D D P Y E H N N
S Q O M R X O A M M N N H P P N B W U M
L G U S R S Q R R E A D F D I E O W T L
J D R K C V E E C Z C O W Z R L X O C N
M Q N D H H H A L H K G A C C B E A I H
U K E P T B J R T P R G W A V Q K U M F
S X Y O R E D T S L A W D L A E R A Y B
H H M R R D P H H M B L K F S C H O O L
```

BARK	HUMMED	RUIN
BIBLE	HUNT	SAUSAGES
BOX	JOURNEY	SCHOOL
CAKE	KERNEL	SHARECROPPERS
CALF	LANTERN	SHERIFF
CHILDREN	LAW	SHOTGUN
CHRISTMAS	MAGAZINES	SOUNDER
COONDOG	MOTHER	SOWBELLY
CRIPPLED	MUSH	STEAL
CURTAINS	NICKS	TEACHER
DIE	PILLOWCASE	TO
EAR	PORCH	TWO
EARTH	PREACHER	WALNUT
FATHER	READ	WOODPILE
HAM	REAL	
HAND	RED	

Sounder Word Search 3 Answer Key

BARK	HUMMED	RUIN
BIBLE	HUNT	SAUSAGES
BOX	JOURNEY	SCHOOL
CAKE	KERNEL	SHARECROPPERS
CALF	LANTERN	SHERIFF
CHILDREN	LAW	SHOTGUN
CHRISTMAS	MAGAZINES	SOUNDER
COONDOG	MOTHER	SOWBELLY
CRIPPLED	MUSH	STEAL
CURTAINS	NICKS	TEACHER
DIE	PILLOWCASE	TO
EAR	PORCH	TWO
EARTH	PREACHER	WALNUT
FATHER	READ	WOODPILE
HAM	REAL	
HAND	RED	

Sounder Word Search 4

```
W A L N U T D N I C K S B Q B K S X M D
O S P Q F E H Z C N V L P F I G A Q A B
O G C R M F N H Q K B N S C B M U G G J
D W J M P I L L O W C A S E L H S P A M
P G U G S D X H Z Z M F T H E R A R Z B
I H F H L X G Z K G B C X S F S G E I T
L V T E C Y D V Q Z G Z Q B W X E A N M
E C K Y S R E P P O R C E R A H S C E H
D A G C G M I L D M F T C F L S N H S F
C J N H T K Q P L P C C U S R C G E F X
L T J R V R E J P N R O T Q F H K R C Y
W A W I P M X R I L D O E H O P H T H
F Y N S O O K U N R E N A Q A O I R Y J
H L S T B A R K R E A D I E M L A E T S
L L H M E V L C E H L O N K D E N D H R
Q E E A T R B Z H T E G S R L R L N A S
R B R S H U N T C A A T E M U D A U N G
W W I L B J W H A F R N S O T D W O D B
J O F Z K W D T E W T S J N G W T S Y B
M S F Z H N U G T O H S C A L F O T J K
```

BARK
BIBLE
BOX
CAKE
CALF
CHILDREN
CHRISTMAS
COONDOG
CRIPPLED
CURTAINS
DIE
EAR
EARTH
FATHER
HAM
HAND

HUMMED
HUNT
JOURNEY
KERNEL
LANTERN
LAW
MAGAZINES
MOTHER
MUSH
NICKS
PILLOWCASE
PORCH
PREACHER
READ
REAL
RED

RUIN
SAUSAGES
SCHOOL
SHARECROPPERS
SHERIFF
SHOTGUN
SOUNDER
SOWBELLY
STEAL
TEACHER
TO
TWO
WALNUT
WOODPILE

Sounder Word Serch 4 Answer Key

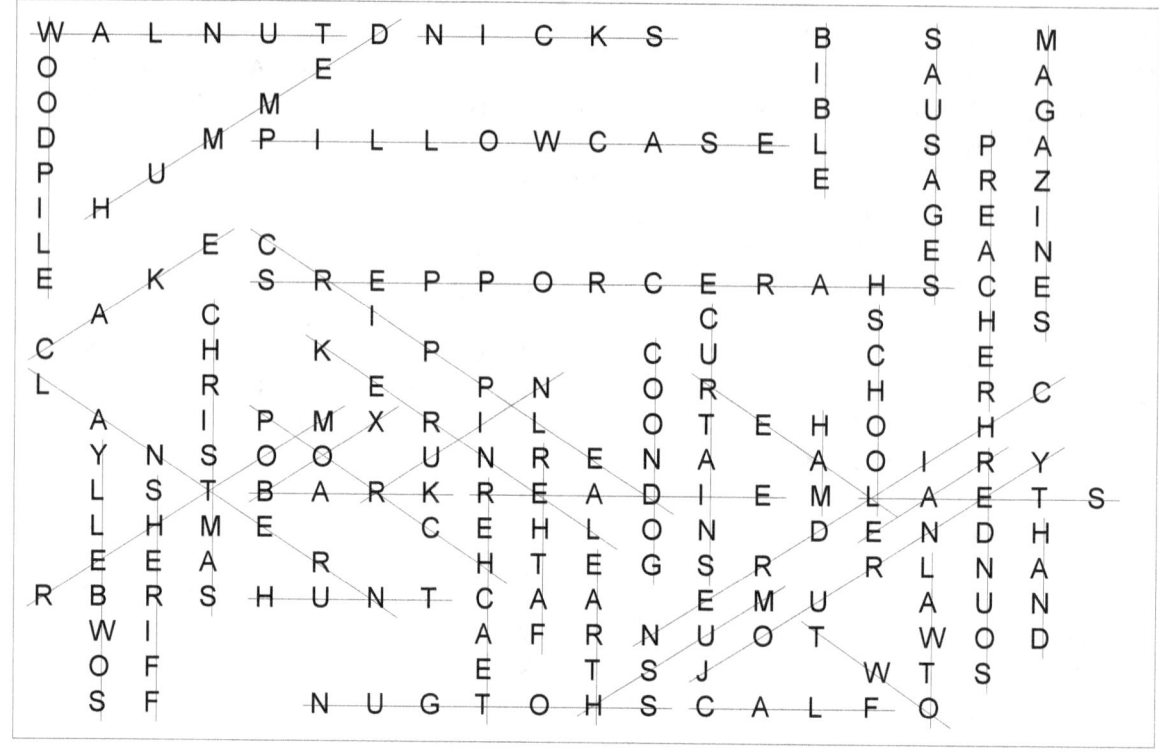

BARK	HUMMED	RUIN
BIBLE	HUNT	SAUSAGES
BOX	JOURNEY	SCHOOL
CAKE	KERNEL	SHARECROPPERS
CALF	LANTERN	SHERIFF
CHILDREN	LAW	SHOTGUN
CHRISTMAS	MAGAZINES	SOUNDER
COONDOG	MOTHER	SOWBELLY
CRIPPLED	MUSH	STEAL
CURTAINS	NICKS	TEACHER
DIE	PILLOWCASE	TO
EAR	PORCH	TWO
EARTH	PREACHER	WALNUT
FATHER	READ	WOODPILE
HAM	REAL	
HAND	RED	

Sounder Crossword 1

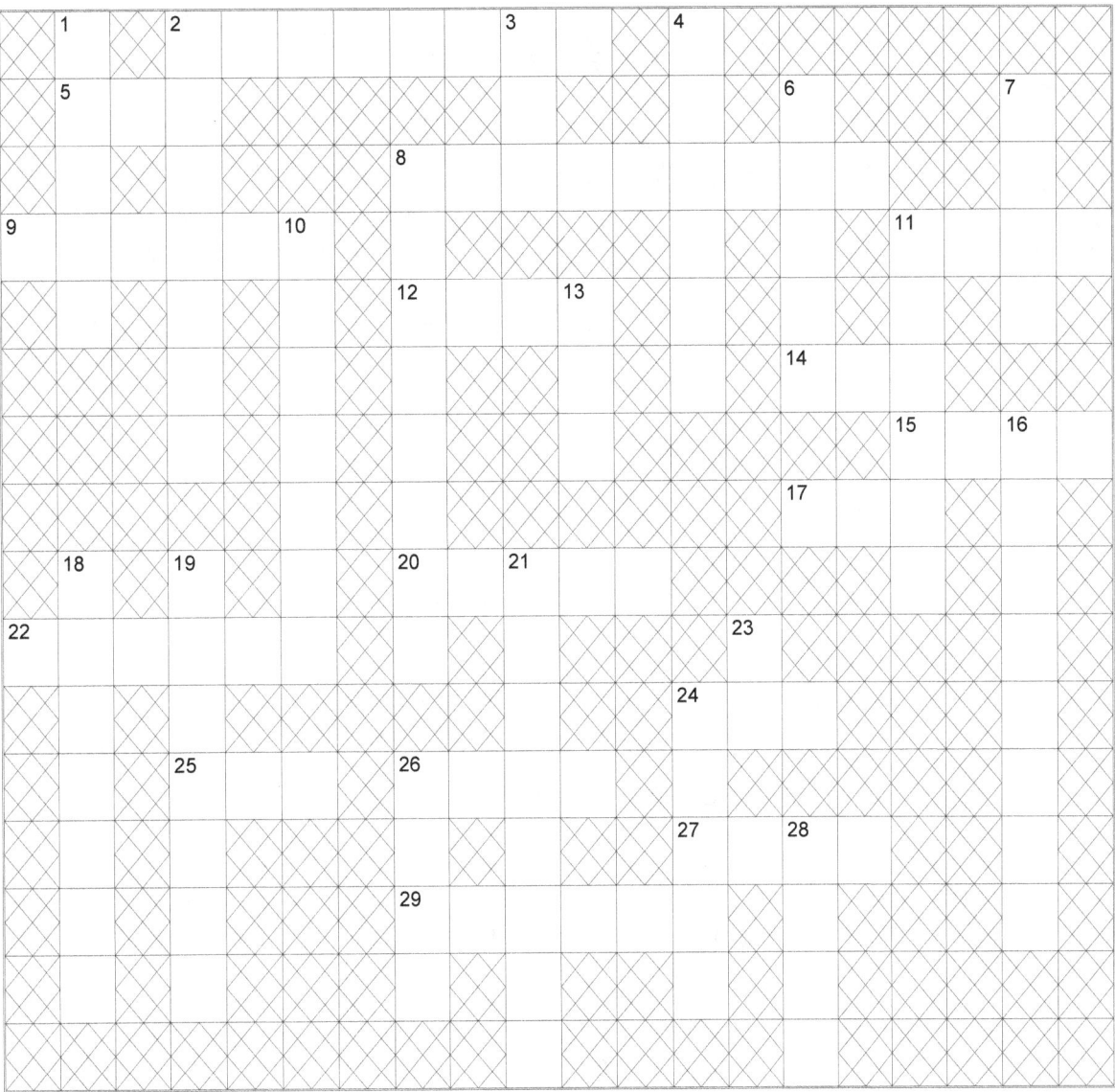

Across
2. What Sounder and Father became
5. Sounder was away for ____ months
8. Holiday season
9. The mother picked these kernels
11. The boy's hurt appendage
12. Actual; true; not imagined
14. The stolen kind of meat
15. What the family ate when they did not have meat
17. Stop living
20. Small cuts and gouges
22. She returned the stolen meat
24. They put the cake in one
25. The ____ faced man at the jail
26. Bottom part of the leg
27. Upon his return, Sounder would not ____; he would only whine
29. Nut meat

Down
1. To take something that isn't yours
2. Sounder was one of these
3. The boy found Sounder's
4. He was sent to a labor camp
6. Dirt; our planet
7. Look for animals to shoot
8. Eyes watched from behind these
10. Instructor
11. What Mother did when she worried
13. Police enforce it
16. Mother returned the pork____
18. A trip
19. County law enforcer
21. The boy's mother told him not to leave them alone
23. The father went ____ jail
24. Book with stories the boy liked
26. Mother baked one for Father
28. The boy wanted to do this

Sounder Crossword 1 Answer Key

	1 S	2 C	R	I	P	P	L	3 E	D		4 F			
	5 T	W	O					A			A		6 E		7 H
	E		O			8 C	H	R	I	S	T	M	A	S	U
9 W	A	L	N	U	10 T	U					H		R		11 H	A	N	D
	L		D		E			12 R	E	13 L			E		U			T
			O		A			T		A			R		14 H	A	M
			G		C			A		W					15 M	U	16 S	H
					H			I					17 D	I	E		A	
	18 J	19 S		20 N	21 C	K	S						D			U
22 M	O	T	H	E	R		S		H			23 T				S
	U		E				I			24 B	O	X				A
	R	25 R	E	D		26 C	A	L	F		I					G
	N		I				A		D		27 B	28 A	R	K		E
	E		F			29 K	E	R	N	E	L		E			S
	Y		F				E		E				A			
							N				D			

Across
2. What Sounder and Father became
5. Sounder was away for ____ months
8. Holiday season
9. The mother picked these kernels
11. The boy's hurt appendage
12. Actual; true; not imagined
14. The stolen kind of meat
15. What the family ate when they did not have meat
17. Stop living
20. Small cuts and gouges
22. She returned the stolen meat
24. They put the cake in one
25. The ____ faced man at the jail
26. Bottom part of the leg
27. Upon his return, Sounder would not ____; he would only whine
29. Nut meat

Down
1. To take something that isn't yours
2. Sounder was one of these
3. The boy found Sounder's
4. He was sent to a labor camp
6. Dirt; our planet
7. Look for animals to shoot
8. Eyes watched from behind these
10. Instructor
11. What Mother did when she worried
13. Police enforce it
16. Mother returned the pork____
18. A trip
19. County law enforcer
21. The boy's mother told him not to leave them alone
23. The father went ____ jail
24. Book with stories the boy liked
26. Mother baked one for Father
28. The boy wanted to do this

Sounder Crossword 2

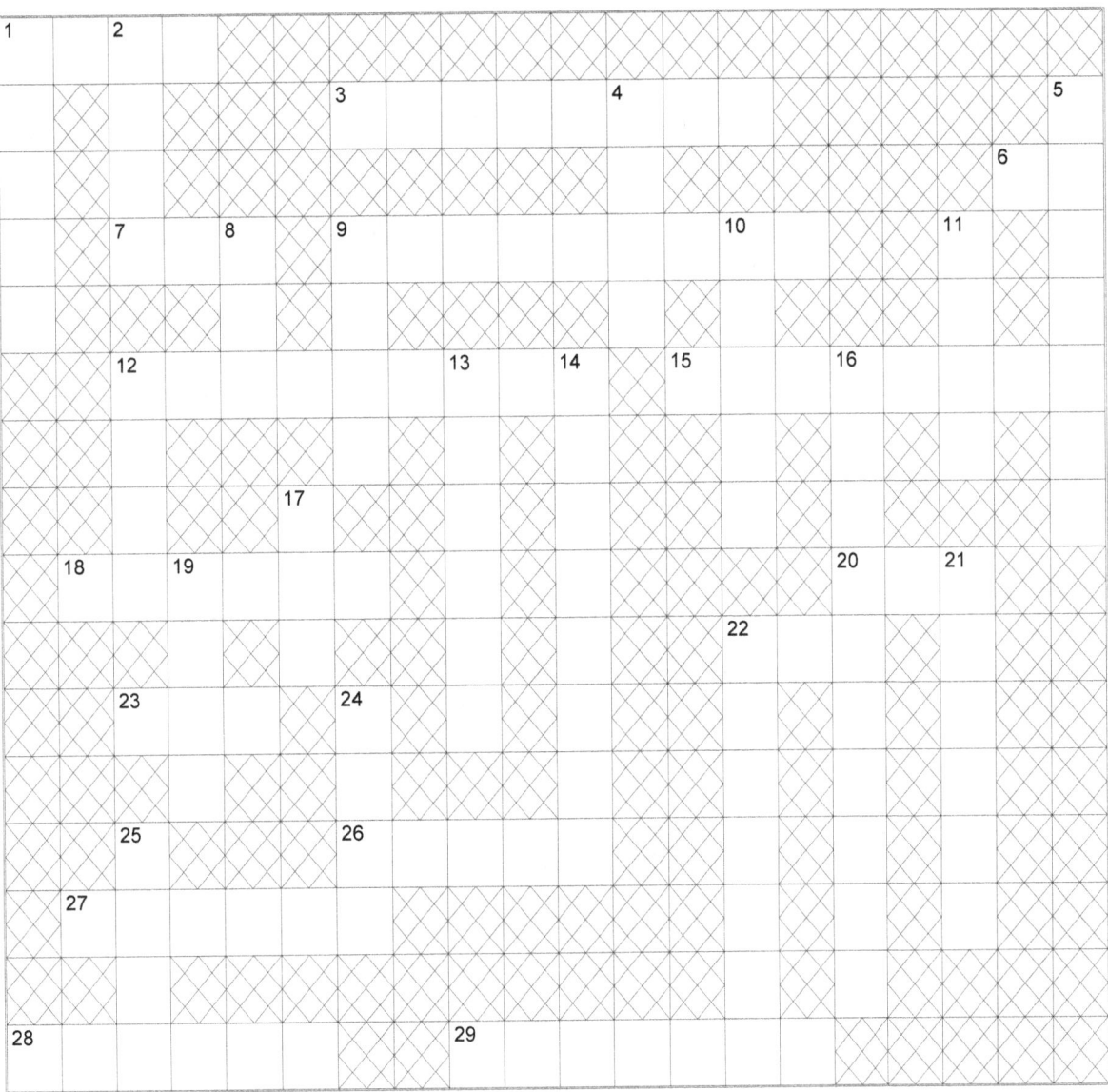

Across
1. Upon his return, Sounder would not ____; he would only whine
3. The boy's mother told him not to leave them alone
6. The father went ____ jail
7. Stop living
9. The boy found these to read
12. Holiday season
15. What Sounder and Father became
18. Nut meat
20. Police enforce it
22. Sounder was away for ____ months
23. The stolen kind of meat
26. Small cuts and gouges
27. What Mother did when she worried
28. He was sent to a labor camp
29. Lamp; usually has oil fuel

Down
1. Book with stories the boy liked
2. The boy wanted to do this
4. The red-faced man ____ed the cake
5. Sounder was one of these
8. The boy found Sounder's
9. What the family ate when they did not have meat
10. Dirt; our planet
11. Bottom part of the leg
12. Mother baked one for Father
13. She returned the stolen meat
14. Mother returned the pork____
16. This was washed every week
17. The ____ faced man at the jail
19. Actual; true; not imagined
21. The mother picked these kernels
22. Instructor
24. The boy's hurt appendage
25. Look for animals to shoot

Sounder Crossword 2 Answer Key

```
 1B  2A  R  K
  I   E        3C  H  I  L  D  4R  E  N              5C
  B   A                          U                6T  O
  L  7D  8I  9E  M  A  G  A  Z  I  N  E  S   11C     O
  E   I   A   U              N         A          N
     12C  H   R  I  S  T  13M  A  14S  15C  R  I  16P  P  L  E  D
      A       H     O     A   T            I     F     O
      K    17R              T     U        H     L     G
   18K  19E  R  N  E  L     H     S              20L  21W
      E       D              E     A        22T  W   O   A
     23H  A   M    24H  R  G  E                W   C   L
      L       A          E     A                    N
     25H      26N  I  C  K  S     C           A   U
     27H  U   M  M  E  D           H           S   T
      N                                            E    E
  28F  A  T   H  E  R        29L  A  N  T  E  R  N
```

Across
1. Upon his return, Sounder would not ____; he would only whine
3. The boy's mother told him not to leave them alone
6. The father went ____ jail
7. Stop living
9. The boy found these to read
12. Holiday season
15. What Sounder and Father became
18. Nut meat
20. Police enforce it
22. Sounder was away for ____ months
23. The stolen kind of meat
26. Small cuts and gouges
27. What Mother did when she worried
28. He was sent to a labor camp
29. Lamp; usually has oil fuel

Down
1. Book with stories the boy liked
2. The boy wanted to do this
4. The red-faced man ____ed the cake
5. Sounder was one of these
8. The boy found Sounder's
9. What the family ate when they did not have meat
10. Dirt; our planet
11. Bottom part of the leg
12. Mother baked one for Father
13. She returned the stolen meat
14. Mother returned the pork____
16. This was washed every week
17. The ____ faced man at the jail
19. Actual; true; not imagined
21. The mother picked these kernels
22. Instructor
24. The boy's hurt appendage
25. Look for animals to shoot

40
Copyrighted

Sounder Crossword 3

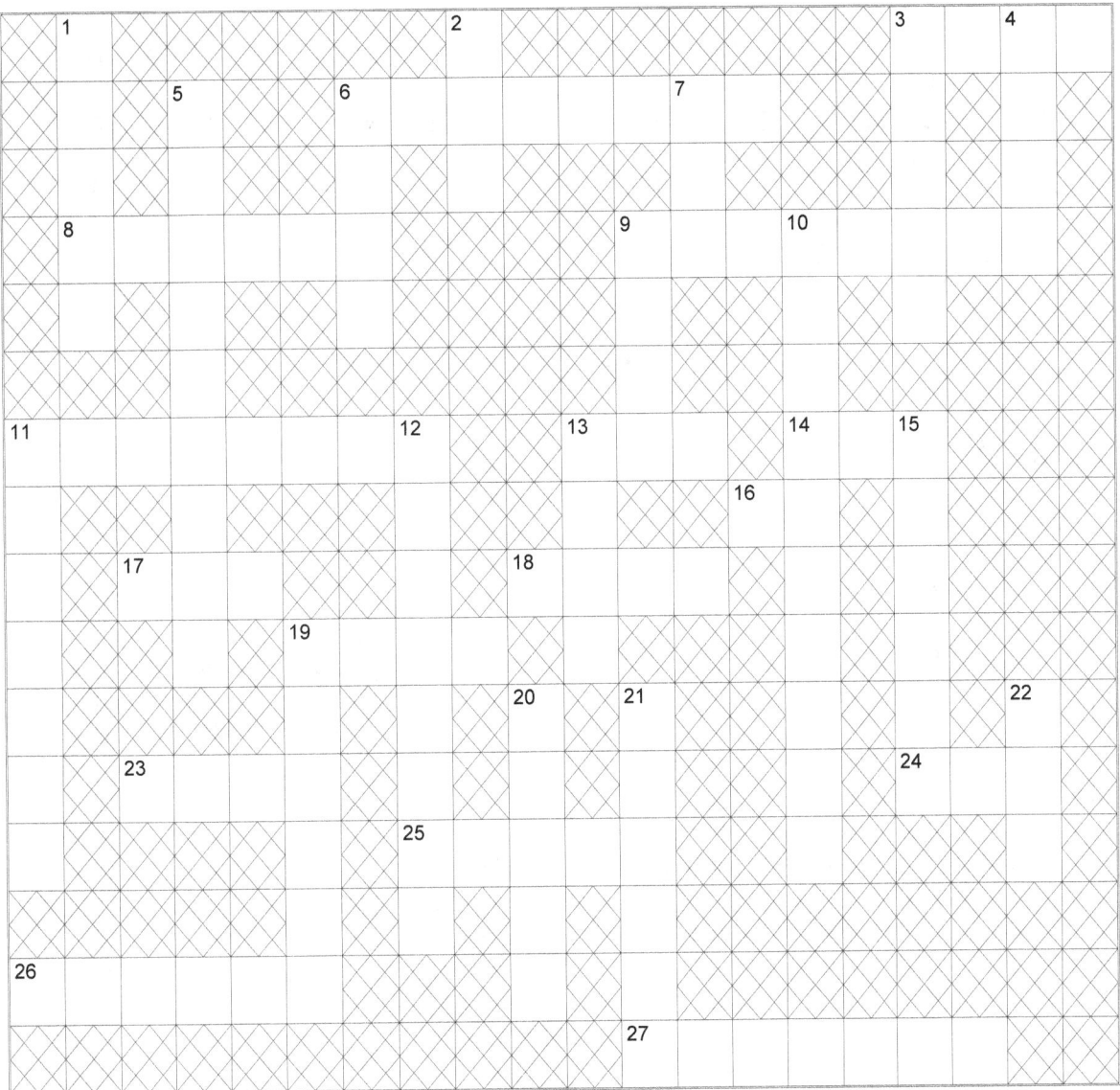

Across
3. Upon his return, Sounder would not ____; he would only whine
6. The boy's mother told him not to leave them alone
8. Nut meat
9. What Sounder and Father became
11. Eyes watched from behind these
13. The ____ faced man at the jail
14. Police enforce it
16. The father went ____ jail
17. The stolen kind of meat
18. The boy's hurt appendage
19. What the family ate when they did not have meat
23. Look for animals to shoot
24. Sounder was away for ____ months
25. Dirt; our planet
26. He was sent to a labor camp
27. Lamp; usually has oil fuel

Down
1. Small cuts and gouges
2. Stop living
3. Book with stories the boy liked
4. The boy wanted to do this
5. Holiday season
6. Bottom part of the leg
7. The boy found Sounder's
9. Mother baked one for Father
10. This was washed every week
11. Sounder was one of these
12. Mother returned the pork____
13. Actual; true; not imagined
15. The mother picked these kernels
19. She returned the stolen meat
20. Sounder crawled under it
21. Place one goes to learn
22. They put the cake in one

SounderCrossword 3 Answer Key

	1		5		6				2			7		3	4	
	N								D					B	A	R	K
	I		C		C	H	I	L	D	R	E	N		I	E	
	C		H		A		E					A		B	A	
8										9			10			
	K	E	R	N	E	L				C	R	I	P	P	L	E	D
	S		I		F					A			I	E		
			S							K			L			
11						12		13				14	15			
C	U	R	T	A	I	N	S		R	E	D		L	A	W	
O			M			A			E			16	T	O	A	
O	17	H	A	M		U		18	H	A	N	D		L		
N			S		19	M	U	S	H		L			C	N	
D						O		A		20	P	21	S		A	22	B
O	23	H	U	N	T		G		O		C			24	U	
G					25	E	A	R	T	H				T	W	O
						E		S		C				E		X
26																
F	A	T	H	E	R			H		O						
								27	L	A	N	T	E	R	N	

Across
3. Upon his return, Sounder would not ____; he would only whine
6. The boy's mother told him not to leave them alone
8. Nut meat
9. What Sounder and Father became
11. Eyes watched from behind these
13. The ____ faced man at the jail
14. Police enforce it
16. The father went ____ jail
17. The stolen kind of meat
18. The boy's hurt appendage
19. What the family ate when they did not have meat
23. Look for animals to shoot
24. Sounder was away for ____ months
25. Dirt; our planet
26. He was sent to a labor camp
27. Lamp; usually has oil fuel

Down
1. Small cuts and gouges
2. Stop living
3. Book with stories the boy liked
4. The boy wanted to do this
5. Holiday season
6. Bottom part of the leg
7. The boy found Sounder's
9. Mother baked one for Father
10. This was washed every week
11. Sounder was one of these
12. Mother returned the pork____
13. Actual; true; not imagined
15. The mother picked these kernels
19. She returned the stolen meat
20. Sounder crawled under it
21. Place one goes to learn
22. They put the cake in one

42
Copyrighted

Sounder Crossword 4

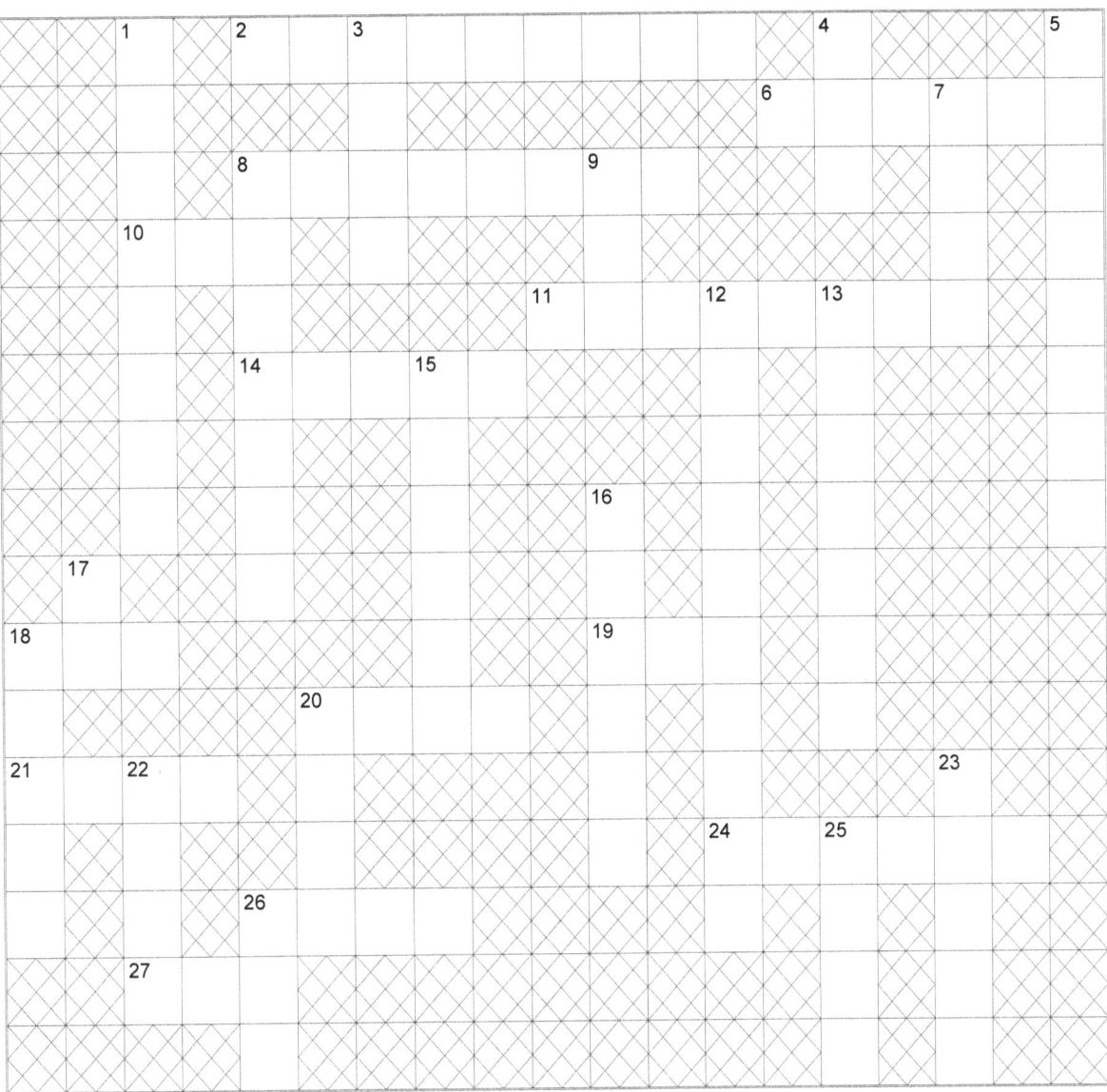

Across
2. Holiday season
6. He was sent to a labor camp
8. The boy's mother told him not to leave them alone
10. Sounder was away for ____ months
11. What Sounder and Father became
14. Small cuts and gouges
18. They put the cake in one
19. Police enforce it
20. Bottom part of the leg
21. Upon his return, Sounder would not ____; he would only whine
24. Place one goes to learn
26. Actual; true; not imagined
27. Stop living

Down
1. Eyes watched from behind these
3. The red-faced man ____ed the cake
4. The stolen kind of meat
5. The father would send word with him
7. The boy's hurt appendage
8. Sounder was one of these
9. The boy found Sounder's
12. This was washed every week
13. Lamp; usually has oil fuel
15. Nut meat
16. The mother picked these kernels
17. The father went ____ jail
18. Book with stories the boy liked
20. Mother baked one for Father
22. The boy wanted to do this
23. Sounder crawled under it
25. Look for animals to shoot
26. The ____ faced man at the jail

Sounder Crossword 4 Answer Key

```
     1       2                        4       5
     C   C H R I S T M A S        H       P
     U       U               6       7
                             F A T H E R
     R   8 C H I L D R E N       M   A   E
     10 T W O   N       9 A           N   A
     A       O           11  12  13
                         C R I P P L E D C
     I   14      15          I   A       H
     N   N I C K S           L   N       E
     N   D       E           L   T       R
     S   O       R       16 W   O       R
     17 T     G       N       A   O   E
     18 B O X         E   19 L A W   R
     I           20 C A L F N   C   N
     21 B 22 A R K   A       U   A   23 P
     L       E       K       T 24 S 25 C H O O L
     E       A   26 R E A L     E   U   R
             27 D I E           N   C
                    D           T   H
```

Across
2. Holiday season
6. He was sent to a labor camp
8. The boy's mother told him not to leave them alone
10. Sounder was away for ____ months
11. What Sounder and Father became
14. Small cuts and gouges
18. They put the cake in one
19. Police enforce it
20. Bottom part of the leg
21. Upon his return, Sounder would not ____; he would only whine
24. Place one goes to learn
26. Actual; true; not imagined
27. Stop living

Down
1. Eyes watched from behind these
3. The red-faced man ____ed the cake
4. The stolen kind of meat
5. The father would send word with him
7. The boy's hurt appendage
8. Sounder was one of these
9. The boy found Sounder's
12. This was washed every week
13. Lamp; usually has oil fuel
15. Nut meat
16. The mother picked these kernels
17. The father went ____ jail
18. Book with stories the boy liked
20. Mother baked one for Father
22. The boy wanted to do this
23. Sounder crawled under it
25. Look for animals to shoot
26. The ____ faced man at the jail

Sounder

SHARECROPPERS	BIBLE	FATHER	SOWBELLY	PILLOWCASE
SHERIFF	CHILDREN	NICKS	EAR	STEAL
LAW	RUIN	FREE SPACE	CRIPPLED	TWO
PORCH	WALNUT	HUNT	BOX	SAUSAGES
READ	HAND	HAM	DIE	TEACHER

Sounder

COONDOG	CAKE	SHOTGUN	REAL	RED
MAGAZINES	SCHOOL	KERNEL	WOODPILE	CHRISTMAS
LANTERN	MUSH	FREE SPACE	TO	JOURNEY
CALF	SOUNDER	HUMMED	PREACHER	BARK
MOTHER	TEACHER	DIE	HAM	HAND

Sounder

HAND	HAM	COONDOG	BARK	FATHER
RED	EAR	HUMMED	WOODPILE	JOURNEY
BIBLE	KERNEL	FREE SPACE	LANTERN	SHOTGUN
CRIPPLED	CHILDREN	TEACHER	RUIN	CHRISTMAS
SOUNDER	READ	PORCH	TWO	WALNUT

Sounder

HUNT	MOTHER	REAL	EARTH	SHARECROPPERS
MUSH	CAKE	SCHOOL	MAGAZINES	STEAL
CURTAINS	TO	FREE SPACE	PILLOWCASE	BOX
LAW	DIE	NICKS	PREACHER	CALF
SOWBELLY	WALNUT	TWO	PORCH	READ

Sounder

SAUSAGES	TO	MOTHER	LANTERN	RUIN
DIE	HUMMED	RED	TWO	JOURNEY
READ	CHILDREN	FREE SPACE	SHOTGUN	SCHOOL
REAL	BARK	EARTH	CURTAINS	HAND
BOX	CHRISTMAS	FATHER	WOODPILE	HUNT

Sounder

COONDOG	PREACHER	NICKS	PILLOWCASE	EAR
SOWBELLY	LAW	SHERIFF	TEACHER	BIBLE
CRIPPLED	PORCH	FREE SPACE	HAM	MUSH
SOUNDER	KERNEL	SHARECROPPERS	STEAL	CAKE
MAGAZINES	HUNT	WOODPILE	FATHER	CHRISTMAS

Sounder

CRIPPLED	REAL	WOODPILE	SAUSAGES	FATHER
CHILDREN	MOTHER	HUNT	HAM	MUSH
RED	RUIN	FREE SPACE	BARK	SHARECROPPERS
PREACHER	BOX	KERNEL	TWO	EARTH
TO	TEACHER	CAKE	BIBLE	SHOTGUN

Sounder

MAGAZINES	COONDOG	LAW	SHERIFF	CALF
HUMMED	NICKS	EAR	DIE	JOURNEY
SCHOOL	HAND	FREE SPACE	PILLOWCASE	CHRISTMAS
PORCH	SOWBELLY	STEAL	CURTAINS	READ
SOUNDER	SHOTGUN	BIBLE	CAKE	TEACHER

Sounder

SOWBELLY	BIBLE	JOURNEY	SOUNDER	READ
CALF	STEAL	CHRISTMAS	WOODPILE	KERNEL
SHERIFF	COONDOG	FREE SPACE	EAR	FATHER
HUMMED	REAL	PILLOWCASE	DIE	LANTERN
PORCH	WALNUT	MAGAZINES	TWO	SHARECROPPERS

Sounder

RUIN	PREACHER	HAM	SCHOOL	SAUSAGES
CURTAINS	MOTHER	BARK	BOX	RED
CAKE	TEACHER	FREE SPACE	MUSH	SHOTGUN
CRIPPLED	EARTH	NICKS	HAND	LAW
TO	SHARECROPPERS	TWO	MAGAZINES	WALNUT

Sounder

LANTERN	BIBLE	HAM	CAKE	CURTAINS
BARK	REAL	PREACHER	FATHER	HUMMED
KERNEL	STEAL	FREE SPACE	LAW	HUNT
TEACHER	NICKS	SOUNDER	TWO	CALF
COONDOG	MAGAZINES	CHILDREN	SHERIFF	EAR

Sounder

TO	HAND	RED	CRIPPLED	JOURNEY
MUSH	WALNUT	PILLOWCASE	READ	MOTHER
SCHOOL	SHARECROPPERS	FREE SPACE	SOWBELLY	CHRISTMAS
BOX	EARTH	DIE	PORCH	RUIN
SHOTGUN	EAR	SHERIFF	CHILDREN	MAGAZINES

Sounder

BARK	MUSH	SHARECROPPERS	CHRISTMAS	EAR
SOUNDER	MOTHER	SOWBELLY	CRIPPLED	BIBLE
TEACHER	PREACHER	FREE SPACE	CHILDREN	EARTH
COONDOG	KERNEL	LANTERN	HUMMED	JOURNEY
DIE	SHOTGUN	RUIN	CURTAINS	HUNT

Sounder

CAKE	STEAL	TWO	SHERIFF	HAND
WALNUT	MAGAZINES	NICKS	PILLOWCASE	LAW
FATHER	SAUSAGES	FREE SPACE	REAL	CALF
BOX	WOODPILE	HAM	PORCH	TO
READ	HUNT	CURTAINS	RUIN	SHOTGUN

Sounder

CHILDREN	TO	MOTHER	EARTH	STEAL
HAM	MAGAZINES	WOODPILE	JOURNEY	EAR
BARK	DIE	FREE SPACE	FATHER	CAKE
READ	PORCH	SOUNDER	SHOTGUN	SCHOOL
RED	HUNT	CHRISTMAS	CRIPPLED	COONDOG

Sounder

SOWBELLY	SHERIFF	SAUSAGES	LAW	CURTAINS
MUSH	NICKS	HAND	HUMMED	KERNEL
TEACHER	PILLOWCASE	FREE SPACE	LANTERN	RUIN
REAL	BOX	PREACHER	WALNUT	CALF
TWO	COONDOG	CRIPPLED	CHRISTMAS	HUNT

Sounder

SOWBELLY	CURTAINS	SHERIFF	HUMMED	BOX
CHRISTMAS	CALF	SHOTGUN	HAM	PREACHER
MOTHER	REAL	FREE SPACE	COONDOG	TWO
LANTERN	RUIN	PORCH	KERNEL	RED
FATHER	PILLOWCASE	SCHOOL	WOODPILE	MUSH

Sounder

SAUSAGES	CHILDREN	MAGAZINES	STEAL	NICKS
TEACHER	CRIPPLED	BIBLE	BARK	SHARECROPPERS
EARTH	SOUNDER	FREE SPACE	EAR	TO
LAW	HUNT	JOURNEY	HAND	DIE
WALNUT	MUSH	WOODPILE	SCHOOL	PILLOWCASE

Sounder

RUIN	PORCH	NICKS	KERNEL	CAKE
WALNUT	BIBLE	SHARECROPPERS	WOODPILE	SAUSAGES
CRIPPLED	BOX	FREE SPACE	TWO	FATHER
CALF	HAM	PREACHER	SOUNDER	LANTERN
STEAL	REAL	RED	PILLOWCASE	MAGAZINES

Sounder

MOTHER	CURTAINS	EARTH	SCHOOL	EAR
SHOTGUN	HUMMED	SOWBELLY	CHRISTMAS	COONDOG
HAND	BARK	FREE SPACE	CHILDREN	READ
TO	HUNT	TEACHER	JOURNEY	DIE
SHERIFF	MAGAZINES	PILLOWCASE	RED	REAL

Sounder

STEAL	NICKS	SCHOOL	PILLOWCASE	KERNEL
MOTHER	BOX	HUMMED	TO	HAND
PORCH	SHARECROPPERS	FREE SPACE	BARK	PREACHER
EAR	MAGAZINES	RUIN	LAW	CURTAINS
TWO	SAUSAGES	EARTH	MUSH	CAKE

Sounder

CRIPPLED	JOURNEY	BIBLE	SOUNDER	WOODPILE
HUNT	CHRISTMAS	SHOTGUN	SHERIFF	SOWBELLY
CHILDREN	DIE	FREE SPACE	LANTERN	REAL
READ	WALNUT	FATHER	CALF	TEACHER
RED	CAKE	MUSH	EARTH	SAUSAGES

Sounder

WOODPILE	PREACHER	DIE	BOX	SCHOOL
EAR	CRIPPLED	TO	HAM	READ
CHILDREN	STEAL	FREE SPACE	REAL	SOWBELLY
JOURNEY	MOTHER	LAW	CURTAINS	HUNT
TWO	BIBLE	COONDOG	PORCH	SHARECROPPERS

Sounder

RUIN	SHERIFF	PILLOWCASE	TEACHER	HAND
MAGAZINES	CHRISTMAS	EARTH	WALNUT	SOUNDER
KERNEL	HUMMED	FREE SPACE	CAKE	SHOTGUN
LANTERN	RED	MUSH	FATHER	CALF
SAUSAGES	SHARECROPPERS	PORCH	COONDOG	BIBLE

Sounder

BOX	BIBLE	TWO	WOODPILE	RUIN
COONDOG	MUSH	PILLOWCASE	SHOTGUN	MOTHER
CHRISTMAS	SCHOOL	FREE SPACE	MAGAZINES	TO
DIE	LANTERN	SOWBELLY	CHILDREN	STEAL
BARK	CAKE	PREACHER	RED	EAR

Sounder

FATHER	READ	CALF	HUMMED	REAL
EARTH	TEACHER	HAND	PORCH	HAM
CURTAINS	SAUSAGES	FREE SPACE	NICKS	KERNEL
SHERIFF	WALNUT	JOURNEY	SOUNDER	HUNT
LAW	EAR	RED	PREACHER	CAKE

Sounder

DIE	PORCH	LAW	WALNUT	SAUSAGES
READ	JOURNEY	NICKS	HAND	MAGAZINES
SOWBELLY	FATHER	FREE SPACE	BIBLE	MUSH
TO	REAL	HAM	KERNEL	SHARECROPPERS
MOTHER	CALF	TWO	EARTH	WOODPILE

Sounder

RUIN	PREACHER	PILLOWCASE	BOX	SHERIFF
CRIPPLED	HUMMED	SCHOOL	SOUNDER	CHRISTMAS
STEAL	CAKE	FREE SPACE	BARK	LANTERN
CHILDREN	HUNT	RED	SHOTGUN	EAR
COONDOG	WOODPILE	EARTH	TWO	CALF

Sounder

TO	JOURNEY	HUNT	RUIN	MOTHER
SHARECROPPERS	PILLOWCASE	RED	EARTH	CALF
BARK	BIBLE	FREE SPACE	LANTERN	EAR
READ	MUSH	CHRISTMAS	HAM	SOWBELLY
COONDOG	WALNUT	MAGAZINES	DIE	PORCH

Sounder

SHOTGUN	SCHOOL	HUMMED	CURTAINS	CHILDREN
TWO	FATHER	WOODPILE	KERNEL	CAKE
SOUNDER	STEAL	FREE SPACE	HAND	LAW
CRIPPLED	SHERIFF	REAL	NICKS	BOX
PREACHER	PORCH	DIE	MAGAZINES	WALNUT

Sounder

BARK	SHERIFF	HUNT	BOX	FATHER
BIBLE	HUMMED	MAGAZINES	LAW	CHRISTMAS
CAKE	PILLOWCASE	FREE SPACE	TEACHER	SOWBELLY
COONDOG	REAL	RED	MUSH	SAUSAGES
EARTH	READ	WALNUT	CURTAINS	CRIPPLED

Sounder

SHOTGUN	KERNEL	WOODPILE	NICKS	JOURNEY
CHILDREN	PREACHER	PORCH	RUIN	DIE
CALF	MOTHER	FREE SPACE	HAM	TWO
TO	LANTERN	HAND	STEAL	SCHOOL
SOUNDER	CRIPPLED	CURTAINS	WALNUT	READ

Sounder Vocabulary Word List

No.	Word	Clue/Definition
1.	ADDLED	Confused
2.	AJAR	Partially opened
3.	ASHEN	Pale
4.	ASKEW	To one side
5.	ASSURED	Made certain; guaranteed; made confident
6.	CALLOUSED	Hardened; toughened
7.	CISTERN	A receptacle for holding water, especially rain water
8.	COMPULSION	An irresistible motivation to do something
9.	CONSTRAINED	Confined; restrained; held back
10.	CURIOSITY	Something that arouses interest
11.	DAMPER	An adjustable plate in the flue of a furnace or stove for controlling the draft
12.	DEFIANT	Boldly resisting
13.	DIM	Lacking brightness or clarity
14.	ENCASED	Enclosed
15.	FAMISHED	Extremely hungry
16.	FRET	Worry
17.	GAUNT	Thin and bony
18.	GLEE	Joy
19.	GRIEVE	Distress; cause to be sorrowful
20.	GYRATIONS	Movements
21.	HESITATED	Paused in uncertainty
22.	INDISTINCT	Unclear
23.	INQUIRING	Asking
24.	JEERED	Taunted; mocked
25.	MINGLED	Mixed
26.	PARCHED	Made dry
27.	PLAINTIVE	Mournful; melancholy
28.	PRECISION	Accuracy; exactness
29.	PUNCTUATED	Interrupted periodically
30.	PURSUIT	The act of chasing after something
31.	QUARRY	Prey; a hunted animal
32.	SUCCESSIVE	Following in uninterrupted order; consecutive
33.	SUFFOCATED	Stifled
34.	TANNERY	Establishment where hides are tanned
35.	TICKING	Mattress or pillow cover made of strong cotton
36.	UNCERTAINTY	Doubtfulness; not knowing for sure
37.	VACCINATE	To give a vaccine to produce an immunity to an infectious disease
38.	VAST	Great in size; huge
39.	VISUALIZED	Formed a mental image
40.	VITALS	Body organs necessary for life
41.	WEARIED	Physically or emotionally tired
42.	WHET	Sharpen

Sounder Vocabulary Fill In The Blank 1

_____

1. Mournful; melancholy

2. Hardened; toughened

3. Made certain; guaranteed; made confident

4. To one side

5. Interrupted periodically

6. Doubtfulness; not knowing for sure

7. Paused in uncertainty

8. The act of chasing after something

9. An irresistible motivation to do something

10. Prey; a hunted animal

11. Mattress or pillow cover made of strong cotton

12. Confused

13. Body organs necessary for life

14. Lacking brightness or clarity

15. Thin and bony

16. Accuracy; exactness

17. Formed a mental image

18. Great in size; huge

19. Taunted; mocked

20. Enclosed

Sounder Vocabulary Fill In The Blank 1 Answer Key

PLAINTIVE	1. Mournful; melancholy
CALLOUSED	2. Hardened; toughened
ASSURED	3. Made certain; guaranteed; made confident
ASKEW	4. To one side
PUNCTUATED	5. Interrupted periodically
UNCERTAINTY	6. Doubtfulness; not knowing for sure
HESITATED	7. Paused in uncertainty
PURSUIT	8. The act of chasing after something
COMPULSION	9. An irresistible motivation to do something
QUARRY	10. Prey; a hunted animal
TICKING	11. Mattress or pillow cover made of strong cotton
ADDLED	12. Confused
VITALS	13. Body organs necessary for life
DIM	14. Lacking brightness or clarity
GAUNT	15. Thin and bony
PRECISION	16. Accuracy; exactness
VISUALIZED	17. Formed a mental image
VAST	18. Great in size; huge
JEERED	19. Taunted; mocked
ENCASED	20. Enclosed

Sounder Vocabulary Fill In The Blank 2

_____ 1. Hardened; toughened

_____ 2. Something that arouses interest

_____ 3. Worry

_____ 4. Accuracy; exactness

_____ 5. Stifled

_____ 6. Lacking brightness or clarity

_____ 7. Partially opened

_____ 8. Paused in uncertainty

_____ 9. An adjustable plate in the flue of a furnace or stove for controlling the draft

_____ 10. Confined; restrained; held back

_____ 11. To give a vaccine to produce an immunity to an infectious disease

_____ 12. Interrupted periodically

_____ 13. Distress; cause to be sorrowful

_____ 14. Asking

_____ 15. Sharpen

_____ 16. An irresistible motivation to do something

_____ 17. Pale

_____ 18. Great in size; huge

_____ 19. Boldly resisting

_____ 20. Physically or emotionally tired

Sounder Vocabulary Fill In The Blank 2 Answer Key

CALLOUSED	1. Hardened; toughened
CURIOSITY	2. Something that arouses interest
FRET	3. Worry
PRECISION	4. Accuracy; exactness
SUFFOCATED	5. Stifled
DIM	6. Lacking brightness or clarity
AJAR	7. Partially opened
HESITATED	8. Paused in uncertainty
DAMPER	9. An adjustable plate in the flue of a furnace or stove for controlling the draft
CONSTRAINED	10. Confined; restrained; held back
VACCINATE	11. To give a vaccine to produce an immunity to an infectious disease
PUNCTUATED	12. Interrupted periodically
GRIEVE	13. Distress; cause to be sorrowful
INQUIRING	14. Asking
WHET	15. Sharpen
COMPULSION	16. An irresistible motivation to do something
ASHEN	17. Pale
VAST	18. Great in size; huge
DEFIANT	19. Boldly resisting
WEARIED	20. Physically or emotionally tired

Sounder Vocabulary Fill In The Blanks 3

1. To one side
2. Worry
3. An adjustable plate in the flue of a furnace or stove for controlling the draft
4. Extremely hungry
5. Mournful; melancholy
6. Stifled
7. Partially opened
8. Doubtfulness; not knowing for sure
9. The act of chasing after something
10. To give a vaccine to produce an immunity to an infectious disease
11. Paused in uncertainty
12. Enclosed
13. Prey; a hunted animal
14. Something that arouses interest
15. A receptacle for holding water, especially rain water
16. Hardened; toughened
17. Movements
18. Establishment where hides are tanned
19. Accuracy; exactness
20. Sharpen

Sounder Vocabulary Fill In The Blanks 3 Answer Key

ASKEW	1.	To one side
FRET	2.	Worry
DAMPER	3.	An adjustable plate in the flue of a furnace or stove for controlling the draft
FAMISHED	4.	Extremely hungry
PLAINTIVE	5.	Mournful; melancholy
SUFFOCATED	6.	Stifled
AJAR	7.	Partially opened
UNCERTAINTY	8.	Doubtfulness; not knowing for sure
PURSUIT	9.	The act of chasing after something
VACCINATE	10.	To give a vaccine to produce an immunity to an infectious disease
HESITATED	11.	Paused in uncertainty
ENCASED	12.	Enclosed
QUARRY	13.	Prey; a hunted animal
CURIOSITY	14.	Something that arouses interest
CISTERN	15.	A receptacle for holding water, especially rain water
CALLOUSED	16.	Hardened; toughened
GYRATIONS	17.	Movements
TANNERY	18.	Establishment where hides are tanned
PRECISION	19.	Accuracy; exactness
WHET	20.	Sharpen

Sounder Vocabulary Fill In The Blank 4

_____ 1. Great in size; huge

_____ 2. Boldly resisting

_____ 3. Partially opened

_____ 4. Sharpen

_____ 5. Movements

_____ 6. Unclear

_____ 7. Taunted; mocked

_____ 8. Interrupted periodically

_____ 9. Confined; restrained; held back

_____ 10. Mattress or pillow cover made of strong cotton

_____ 11. An adjustable plate in the flue of a furnace or stove for controlling the draft

_____ 12. Worry

_____ 13. Mixed

_____ 14. To one side

_____ 15. Confused

_____ 16. To give a vaccine to produce an immunity to an infectious disease

_____ 17. Enclosed

_____ 18. Stifled

_____ 19. Asking

_____ 20. Accuracy; exactness

Sounder Vocabulary Fill In The Blank 4 Answer Key

VAST	1. Great in size; huge
DEFIANT	2. Boldly resisting
AJAR	3. Partially opened
WHET	4. Sharpen
GYRATIONS	5. Movements
INDISTINCT	6. Unclear
JEERED	7. Taunted; mocked
PUNCTUATED	8. Interrupted periodically
CONSTRAINED	9. Confined; restrained; held back
TICKING	10. Mattress or pillow cover made of strong cotton
DAMPER	11. An adjustable plate in the flue of a furnace or stove for controlling the draft
FRET	12. Worry
MINGLED	13. Mixed
ASKEW	14. To one side
ADDLED	15. Confused
VACCINATE	16. To give a vaccine to produce an immunity to an infectious disease
ENCASED	17. Enclosed
SUFFOCATED	18. Stifled
INQUIRING	19. Asking
PRECISION	20. Accuracy; exactness

Sounder Vocabulary Matching 1

___ 1. PURSUIT   A. Mixed
___ 2. DIM   B. The act of chasing after something
___ 3. QUARRY   C. An adjustable plate in the flue of a furnace or stove for controlling the draft
___ 4. PARCHED   D. Partially opened
___ 5. ENCASED   E. An irresistible motivation to do something
___ 6. MINGLED   F. Enclosed
___ 7. INDISTINCT   G. Confused
___ 8. CONSTRAINED   H. Joy
___ 9. GYRATIONS   I. Following in uninterrupted order; consecutive
___10. GLEE   J. Movements
___11. DAMPER   K. Lacking brightness or clarity
___12. WEARIED   L. A receptacle for holding water, especially rain water
___13. ASHEN   M. Extremely hungry
___14. FAMISHED   N. Accuracy; exactness
___15. COMPULSION   O. To give a vaccine to produce an immunity to an infectious disease
___16. AJAR   P. To one side
___17. UNCERTAINTY   Q. Doubtfulness; not knowing for sure
___18. CISTERN   R. Physically or emotionally tired
___19. DEFIANT   S. Pale
___20. VACCINATE   T. Distress; cause to be sorrowful
___21. GRIEVE   U. Prey; a hunted animal
___22. ASKEW   V. Unclear
___23. PRECISION   W. Confined; restrained; held back
___24. SUCCESSIVE   X. Boldly resisting
___25. ADDLED   Y. Made dry

Sounder Vocabulary Matching 1 Answer Key

- B - 1. PURSUIT
- K - 2. DIM
- U - 3. QUARRY
- Y - 4. PARCHED
- F - 5. ENCASED
- A - 6. MINGLED
- V - 7. INDISTINCT
- W - 8. CONSTRAINED
- J - 9. GYRATIONS
- H - 10. GLEE
- C - 11. DAMPER
- R - 12. WEARIED
- S - 13. ASHEN
- M - 14. FAMISHED
- E - 15. COMPULSION
- D - 16. AJAR
- Q - 17. UNCERTAINTY
- L - 18. CISTERN
- X - 19. DEFIANT
- O - 20. VACCINATE
- T - 21. GRIEVE
- P - 22. ASKEW
- N - 23. PRECISION
- I - 24. SUCCESSIVE
- G - 25. ADDLED

A. Mixed
B. The act of chasing after something
C. An adjustable plate in the flue of a furnace or stove for controlling the draft
D. Partially opened
E. An irresistible motivation to do something
F. Enclosed
G. Confused
H. Joy
I. Following in uninterrupted order; consecutive
J. Movements
K. Lacking brightness or clarity
L. A receptacle for holding water, especially rain water
M. Extremely hungry
N. Accuracy; exactness
O. To give a vaccine to produce an immunity to an infectious disease
P. To one side
Q. Doubtfulness; not knowing for sure
R. Physically or emotionally tired
S. Pale
T. Distress; cause to be sorrowful
U. Prey; a hunted animal
V. Unclear
W. Confined; restrained; held back
X. Boldly resisting
Y. Made dry

Sounder Vocabulary Matching 2

___ 1. QUARRY   A. Body organs necessary for life
___ 2. ASSURED   B. Mattress or pillow cover made of strong cotton
___ 3. PRECISION   C. Taunted; mocked
___ 4. PARCHED   D. An irresistible motivation to do something
___ 5. UNCERTAINTY   E. Paused in uncertainty
___ 6. VISUALIZED   F. Made dry
___ 7. SUCCESSIVE   G. Extremely hungry
___ 8. GLEE   H. To give a vaccine to produce an immunity to an infectious disease
___ 9. HESITATED   I. An adjustable plate in the flue of a furnace or stove for controlling the draft
___10. COMPULSION   J. Distress; cause to be sorrowful
___11. GRIEVE   K. Mixed
___12. GYRATIONS   L. Doubtfulness; not knowing for sure
___13. CALLOUSED   M. Formed a mental image
___14. DAMPER   N. Made certain; guaranteed; made confident
___15. MINGLED   O. Confined; restrained; held back
___16. VACCINATE   P. Establishment where hides are tanned
___17. JEERED   Q. Enclosed
___18. CONSTRAINED   R. Following in uninterrupted order; consecutive
___19. TICKING   S. Accuracy; exactness
___20. TANNERY   T. Joy
___21. VITALS   U. Hardened; toughened
___22. ENCASED   V. Physically or emotionally tired
___23. FAMISHED   W. Movements
___24. WEARIED   X. Stifled
___25. SUFFOCATED   Y. Prey; a hunted animal

Sounder Vocabulary Matching 2 Answer Key

Y - 1.	QUARRY	A. Body organs necessary for life
N - 2.	ASSURED	B. Mattress or pillow cover made of strong cotton
S - 3.	PRECISION	C. Taunted; mocked
F - 4.	PARCHED	D. An irresistible motivation to do something
L - 5.	UNCERTAINTY	E. Paused in uncertainty
M - 6.	VISUALIZED	F. Made dry
R - 7.	SUCCESSIVE	G. Extremely hungry
T - 8.	GLEE	H. To give a vaccine to produce an immunity to an infectious disease
E - 9.	HESITATED	I. An adjustable plate in the flue of a furnace or stove for controlling the draft
D -10.	COMPULSION	J. Distress; cause to be sorrowful
J -11.	GRIEVE	K. Mixed
W -12.	GYRATIONS	L. Doubtfulness; not knowing for sure
U -13.	CALLOUSED	M. Formed a mental image
I -14.	DAMPER	N. Made certain; guaranteed; made confident
K -15.	MINGLED	O. Confined; restrained; held back
H -16.	VACCINATE	P. Establishment where hides are tanned
C -17.	JEERED	Q. Enclosed
O -18.	CONSTRAINED	R. Following in uninterrupted order; consecutive
B -19.	TICKING	S. Accuracy; exactness
P -20.	TANNERY	T. Joy
A -21.	VITALS	U. Hardened; toughened
Q -22.	ENCASED	V. Physically or emotionally tired
G -23.	FAMISHED	W. Movements
V -24.	WEARIED	X. Stifled
X -25.	SUFFOCATED	Y. Prey; a hunted animal

Sounder Vocabulary Matching 3

___ 1. ENCASED   A. Mattress or pillow cover made of strong cotton
___ 2. VACCINATE   B. Hardened; toughened
___ 3. TANNERY   C. Enclosed
___ 4. SUFFOCATED   D. Mournful; melancholy
___ 5. PURSUIT   E. Sharpen
___ 6. GLEE   F. Confused
___ 7. ASHEN   G. Formed a mental image
___ 8. TICKING   H. Joy
___ 9. CALLOUSED   I. Partially opened
___10. PARCHED   J. Prey; a hunted animal
___11. WHET   K. Stifled
___12. ADDLED   L. Physically or emotionally tired
___13. CONSTRAINED   M. The act of chasing after something
___14. VISUALIZED   N. Movements
___15. ASSURED   O. Establishment where hides are tanned
___16. ASKEW   P. Distress; cause to be sorrowful
___17. INDISTINCT   Q. Pale
___18. GYRATIONS   R. To give a vaccine to produce an immunity to an infectious disease
___19. SUCCESSIVE   S. Unclear
___20. VAST   T. Following in uninterrupted order; consecutive
___21. GRIEVE   U. Confined; restrained; held back
___22. PLAINTIVE   V. To one side
___23. AJAR   W. Made dry
___24. QUARRY   X. Great in size; huge
___25. WEARIED   Y. Made certain; guaranteed; made confident

Sounder Vocabulary Matching 3 Answer Key

C - 1. ENCASED
R - 2. VACCINATE
O - 3. TANNERY
K - 4. SUFFOCATED
M - 5. PURSUIT
H - 6. GLEE
Q - 7. ASHEN
A - 8. TICKING
B - 9. CALLOUSED
W - 10. PARCHED
E - 11. WHET
F - 12. ADDLED
U - 13. CONSTRAINED
G - 14. VISUALIZED
Y - 15. ASSURED
V - 16. ASKEW
S - 17. INDISTINCT
N - 18. GYRATIONS
T - 19. SUCCESSIVE
X - 20. VAST
P - 21. GRIEVE
D - 22. PLAINTIVE
I - 23. AJAR
J - 24. QUARRY
L - 25. WEARIED

A. Mattress or pillow cover made of strong cotton
B. Hardened; toughened
C. Enclosed
D. Mournful; melancholy
E. Sharpen
F. Confused
G. Formed a mental image
H. Joy
I. Partially opened
J. Prey; a hunted animal
K. Stifled
L. Physically or emotionally tired
M. The act of chasing after something
N. Movements
O. Establishment where hides are tanned
P. Distress; cause to be sorrowful
Q. Pale
R. To give a vaccine to produce an immunity to an infectious disease
S. Unclear
T. Following in uninterrupted order; consecutive
U. Confined; restrained; held back
V. To one side
W. Made dry
X. Great in size; huge
Y. Made certain; guaranteed; made confident

Sounder Vocabulary Matching 4

___ 1. SUCCESSIVE   A. Boldly resisting
___ 2. PURSUIT   B. Taunted; mocked
___ 3. ASHEN   C. Joy
___ 4. GLEE   D. Formed a mental image
___ 5. FRET   E. Prey; a hunted animal
___ 6. CONSTRAINED   F. Extremely hungry
___ 7. DEFIANT   G. Worry
___ 8. GAUNT   H. The act of chasing after something
___ 9. GRIEVE   I. Confused
___10. JEERED   J. Thin and bony
___11. PARCHED   K. Enclosed
___12. VISUALIZED   L. To one side
___13. UNCERTAINTY   M. A receptacle for holding water, especially rain water
___14. INDISTINCT   N. Distress; cause to be sorrowful
___15. AJAR   O. Partially opened
___16. ASSURED   P. Mattress or pillow cover made of strong cotton
___17. ASKEW   Q. Doubtfulness; not knowing for sure
___18. ENCASED   R. Pale
___19. TICKING   S. Made certain; guaranteed; made confident
___20. FAMISHED   T. Mournful; melancholy
___21. CISTERN   U. Made dry
___22. QUARRY   V. Mixed
___23. ADDLED   W. Following in uninterrupted order; consecutive
___24. MINGLED   X. Confined; restrained; held back
___25. PLAINTIVE   Y. Unclear

Sounder Vocabulary Matching 4 Answer Key

W	1. SUCCESSIVE	A.	Boldly resisting
H	2. PURSUIT	B.	Taunted; mocked
R	3. ASHEN	C.	Joy
C	4. GLEE	D.	Formed a mental image
G	5. FRET	E.	Prey; a hunted animal
X	6. CONSTRAINED	F.	Extremely hungry
A	7. DEFIANT	G.	Worry
J	8. GAUNT	H.	The act of chasing after something
N	9. GRIEVE	I.	Confused
B	10. JEERED	J.	Thin and bony
U	11. PARCHED	K.	Enclosed
D	12. VISUALIZED	L.	To one side
Q	13. UNCERTAINTY	M.	A receptacle for holding water, especially rain water
Y	14. INDISTINCT	N.	Distress; cause to be sorrowful
O	15. AJAR	O.	Partially opened
S	16. ASSURED	P.	Mattress or pillow cover made of strong cotton
L	17. ASKEW	Q.	Doubtfulness; not knowing for sure
K	18. ENCASED	R.	Pale
P	19. TICKING	S.	Made certain; guaranteed; made confident
F	20. FAMISHED	T.	Mournful; melancholy
M	21. CISTERN	U.	Made dry
E	22. QUARRY	V.	Mixed
I	23. ADDLED	W.	Following in uninterrupted order; consecutive
V	24. MINGLED	X.	Confined; restrained; held back
T	25. PLAINTIVE	Y.	Unclear

Sounder Vocabulary Magic Squares 1

Match the definition with the vocabulary word. Put your answers in the magic squares below. When your answers are correct, all columns and rows will add to the same number.

A. PURSUIT
B. GYRATIONS
C. TICKING
D. PARCHED
E. DEFIANT
F. JEERED
G. QUARRY
H. VAST
I. AJAR
J. FAMISHED
K. DAMPER
L. FRET
M. HESITATED
N. DIM
O. SUFFOCATED
P. MINGLED

1. Taunted; mocked
2. Partially opened
3. Stifled
4. Made dry
5. Paused in uncertainty
6. Movements
7. Great in size; huge
8. An adjustable plate in the flue of a furnace or stove for controlling the draft
9. Mattress or pillow cover made of strong cotton
10. Mixed
11. Extremely hungry
12. Boldly resisting
13. Worry
14. Prey; a hunted animal
15. The act of chasing after something
16. Lacking brightness or clarity

A=	B=	C=	D=
E=	F=	G=	H=
I=	J=	K=	L=
M=	N=	O=	P=

Sounder Vocabulary Magic Squares 1 Answer Key

Match the definition with the vocabulary word. Put your answers in the magic squares below. When your answers are correct, all columns and rows will add to the same number.

A. PURSUIT
B. GYRATIONS
C. TICKING
D. PARCHED
E. DEFIANT
F. JEERED
G. QUARRY
H. VAST
I. AJAR
J. FAMISHED
K. DAMPER
L. FRET
M. HESITATED
N. DIM
O. SUFFOCATED
P. MINGLED

1. Taunted; mocked
2. Partially opened
3. Stifled
4. Made dry
5. Paused in uncertainty
6. Movements
7. Great in size; huge
8. An adjustable plate in the flue of a furnace or stove for controlling the draft
9. Mattress or pillow cover made of strong cotton
10. Mixed
11. Extremely hungry
12. Boldly resisting
13. Worry
14. Prey; a hunted animal
15. The act of chasing after something
16. Lacking brightness or clarity

A=15	B=6	C=9	D=4
E=12	F=1	G=14	H=7
I=2	J=11	K=8	L=13
M=5	N=16	O=3	P=10

Sounder Vocabulary Magic Squares 2

Match the definition with the vocabulary word. Put your answers in the magic squares below. When your answers are correct, all columns and rows will add to the same number.

A. ENCASED
B. DIM
C. SUCCESSIVE
D. FAMISHED
E. COMPULSION
F. MINGLED
G. DAMPER
H. UNCERTAINTY
I. CISTERN
J. QUARRY
K. VITALS
L. TICKING
M. GLEE
N. ASHEN
O. HESITATED
P. VACCINATE

1. Lacking brightness or clarity
2. An adjustable plate in the flue of a furnace or stove for controlling the draft
3. Body organs necessary for life
4. Pale
5. Joy
6. Mattress or pillow cover made of strong cotton
7. Doubtfulness; not knowing for sure
8. Enclosed
9. To give a vaccine to produce an immunity to an infectious disease
10. A receptacle for holding water, especially rain water
11. An irresistible motivation to do something
12. Extremely hungry
13. Following in uninterrupted order; consecutive
14. Mixed
15. Prey; a hunted animal
16. Paused in uncertainty

A=	B=	C=	D=
E=	F=	G=	H=
I=	J=	K=	L=
M=	N=	O=	P=

Sounder Vocabulary Magic Squares 2 Answer Key

Match the definition with the vocabulary word. Put your answers in the magic squares below. When your answers are correct, all columns and rows will add to the same number.

A. ENCASED
B. DIM
C. SUCCESSIVE
D. FAMISHED
E. COMPULSION
F. MINGLED
G. DAMPER
H. UNCERTAINTY
I. CISTERN
J. QUARRY
K. VITALS
L. TICKING
M. GLEE
N. ASHEN
O. HESITATED
P. VACCINATE

1. Lacking brightness or clarity
2. An adjustable plate in the flue of a furnace or stove for controlling the draft
3. Body organs necessary for life
4. Pale
5. Joy
6. Mattress or pillow cover made of strong cotton
7. Doubtfulness; not knowing for sure
8. Enclosed
9. To give a vaccine to produce an immunity to an infectious disease
10. A receptacle for holding water, especially rain water
11. An irresistible motivation to do something
12. Extremely hungry
13. Following in uninterrupted order; consecutive
14. Mixed
15. Prey; a hunted animal
16. Paused in uncertainty

A=8	B=1	C=13	D=12
E=11	F=14	G=2	H=7
I=10	J=15	K=3	L=6
M=5	N=4	O=16	P=9

Sounder Vocabulary Magic Squares 3

Match the definition with the vocabulary word. Put your answers in the magic squares below. When your answers are correct, all columns and rows will add to the same number.

A. ENCASED
B. TANNERY
C. FRET
D. PUNCTUATED
E. WHET
F. MINGLED
G. DAMPER
H. CURIOSITY
I. CALLOUSED
J. TICKING
K. PURSUIT
L. JEERED
M. INQUIRING
N. ASHEN
O. SUCCESSIVE
P. ASKEW

1. Enclosed
2. Pale
3. Mattress or pillow cover made of strong cotton
4. Sharpen
5. An adjustable plate in the flue of a furnace or stove for controlling the draft
6. Taunted; mocked
7. To one side
8. Worry
9. Following in uninterrupted order; consecutive
10. Interrupted periodically
11. Something that arouses interest
12. The act of chasing after something
13. Hardened; toughened
14. Mixed
15. Establishment where hides are tanned
16. Asking

A=	B=	C=	D=
E=	F=	G=	H=
I=	J=	K=	L=
M=	N=	O=	P=

Sounder Vocabulary Magic Squares 3 Answer Key

Match the definition with the vocabulary word. Put your answers in the magic squares below. When your answers are correct, all columns and rows will add to the same number.

A. ENCASED
B. TANNERY
C. FRET
D. PUNCTUATED
E. WHET
F. MINGLED
G. DAMPER
H. CURIOSITY
I. CALLOUSED
J. TICKING
K. PURSUIT
L. JEERED
M. INQUIRING
N. ASHEN
O. SUCCESSIVE
P. ASKEW

1. Enclosed
2. Pale
3. Mattress or pillow cover made of strong cotton
4. Sharpen
5. An adjustable plate in the flue of a furnace or stove for controlling the draft
6. Taunted; mocked
7. To one side
8. Worry
9. Following in uninterrupted order; consecutive
10. Interrupted periodically
11. Something that arouses interest
12. The act of chasing after something
13. Hardened; toughened
14. Mixed
15. Establishment where hides are tanned
16. Asking

A=1	B=15	C=8	D=10
E=4	F=14	G=5	H=11
I=13	J=3	K=12	L=6
M=16	N=2	O=9	P=7

Sounder Vocabulary Magic Squares 4

Match the definition with the vocabulary word. Put your answers in the magic squares below. When your answers are correct, all columns and rows will add to the same number.

A. FAMISHED
B. ADDLED
C. TANNERY
D. SUCCESSIVE
E. DIM
F. GAUNT
G. PARCHED
H. GLEE
I. UNCERTAINTY
J. WHET
K. ASHEN
L. CONSTRAINED
M. ASKEW
N. CISTERN
O. PRECISION
P. WEARIED

1. A receptacle for holding water, especially rain water
2. Made dry
3. Confined; restrained; held back
4. Extremely hungry
5. Pale
6. Confused
7. To one side
8. Joy
9. Lacking brightness or clarity
10. Physically or emotionally tired
11. Establishment where hides are tanned
12. Sharpen
13. Following in uninterrupted order; consecutive
14. Doubtfulness; not knowing for sure
15. Thin and bony
16. Accuracy; exactness

A=	B=	C=	D=
E=	F=	G=	H=
I=	J=	K=	L=
M=	N=	O=	P=

Sounder Vocabulary Magic Squares 4 Answer Key

Match the definition with the vocabulary word. Put your answers in the magic squares below. When your answers are correct, all columns and rows will add to the same number.

A. FAMISHED
B. ADDLED
C. TANNERY
D. SUCCESSIVE
E. DIM
F. GAUNT
G. PARCHED
H. GLEE
I. UNCERTAINTY
J. WHET
K. ASHEN
L. CONSTRAINED
M. ASKEW
N. CISTERN
O. PRECISION
P. WEARIED

1. A receptacle for holding water, especially rain water
2. Made dry
3. Confined; restrained; held back
4. Extremely hungry
5. Pale
6. Confused
7. To one side
8. Joy
9. Lacking brightness or clarity
10. Physically or emotionally tired
11. Establishment where hides are tanned
12. Sharpen
13. Following in uninterrupted order; consecutive
14. Doubtfulness; not knowing for sure
15. Thin and bony
16. Accuracy; exactness

A=4	B=6	C=11	D=13
E=9	F=15	G=2	H=8
I=14	J=12	K=5	L=3
M=7	N=1	O=16	P=10

Sounder Vocabulary Word Search 1

```
N W X X C D C U R I O S I T Y M W D C F
D Z F W X A J D R M U A C D F H Y F D P
Y J V Z E B L H S F V I S U A L I Z E D
J Y Z D H A W L F E V I S S E C C U S R
J R C X E P R O O Q F A T B U N T H C K
M R D R S H C I Z U G S D A V R B M S I
X A G B I A F J E L S H C N L R E I N V
P U N C T U A T E D W E N C A S E D F G
Y Q N E A I K E L E V N D J F D I L Z Y
C C D C T T C P Y V R T A Z H S D V B G
I O Q G E P R K A W E E B X T T Z L T B
N M N H D R A S I R C J D I N A R V E D
Q P W S F K T R F N L W N A U N B F N D
U U C P T A P A C B G C I D A N X M M N
I L L U R M X I H T F G A G E Z S R G
R S K R Q Y A I P N E T R M V R C E L H
I I Z S V M P I S D T D I P P Y T D P J
N O T U D S X Y N H C Y E E Z S P G T Z
G N M I N G L E D E E X V R I A S K E W
E V I T N I A L P R D D E C F C H B J H
```

A receptacle for holding water, especially rain water (7)
An adjustable plate in the flue of a furnace or stove for controlling the draft (6)
An irresistible motivation to do something (10)
Asking (9)
Body organs necessary for life (6)
Boldly resisting (7)
Confined; restrained; held back (11)
Confused (6)
Distress; cause to be sorrowful (6)
Doubtfulness; not knowing for sure (11)
Enclosed (7)
Establishment where hides are tanned (7)
Extremely hungry (8)
Following in uninterrupted order; consecutive (10)
Formed a mental image (10)
Great in size; huge (4)
Hardened; toughened (9)
Interrupted periodically (10)
Joy (4)
Lacking brightness or clarity (3)

Made certain; guaranteed; made confident (7)
Made dry (7)
Mattress or pillow cover made of strong cotton (7)
Mixed (7)
Mournful; melancholy (9)
Pale (5)
Partially opened (4)
Paused in uncertainty (9)
Physically or emotionally tired (7)
Prey; a hunted animal (6)
Sharpen (4)
Something that arouses interest (9)
Stifled (10)
Taunted; mocked (6)
The act of chasing after something (7)
Thin and bony (5)
To one side (5)
Unclear (10)
Worry (4)

Sounder Vocabulary Word Search 1 Answer Key

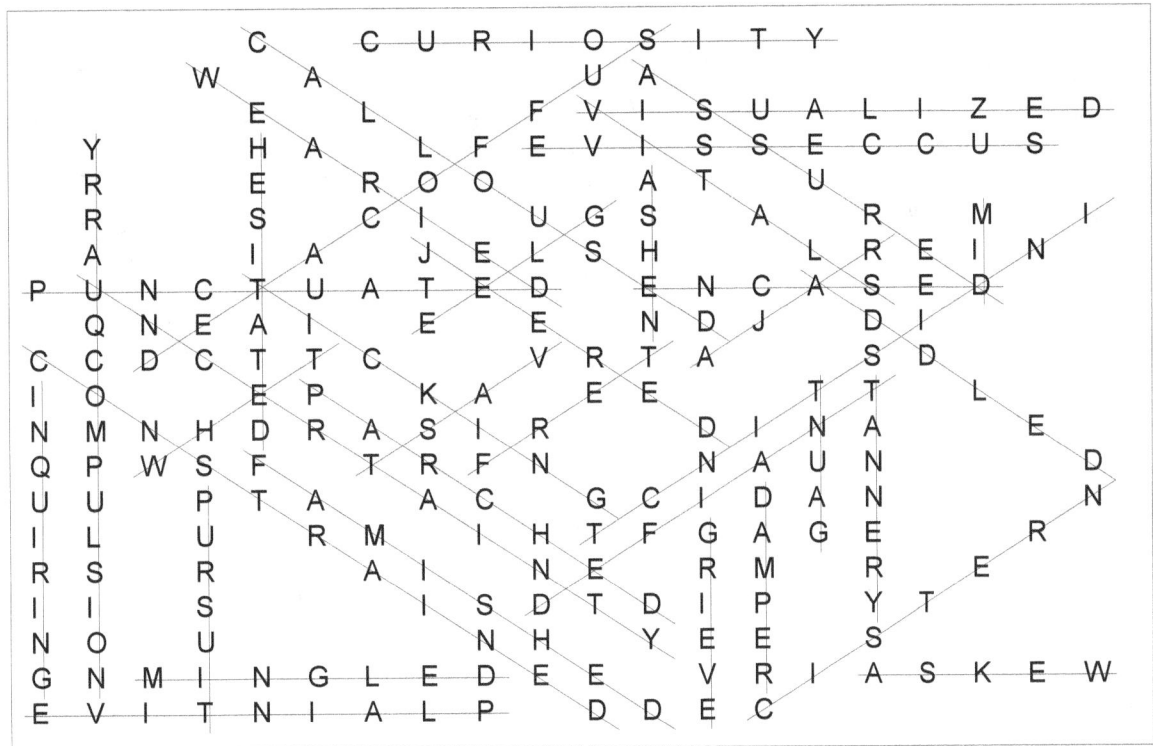

A receptacle for holding water, especially rain water (7)
An adjustable plate in the flue of a furnace or stove for controlling the draft (6)
An irresistible motivation to do something (10)
Asking (9)
Body organs necessary for life (6)
Boldly resisting (7)
Confined; restrained; held back (11)
Confused (6)
Distress; cause to be sorrowful (6)
Doubtfulness; not knowing for sure (11)
Enclosed (7)
Establishment where hides are tanned (7)
Extremely hungry (8)
Following in uninterrupted order; consecutive (10)
Formed a mental image (10)
Great in size; huge (4)
Hardened; toughened (9)
Interrupted periodically (10)
Joy (4)
Lacking brightness or clarity (3)

Made certain; guaranteed; made confident (7)
Made dry (7)
Mattress or pillow cover made of strong cotton (7)
Mixed (7)
Mournful; melancholy (9)
Pale (5)
Partially opened (4)
Paused in uncertainty (9)
Physically or emotionally tired (7)
Prey; a hunted animal (6)
Sharpen (4)
Something that arouses interest (9)
Stifled (10)
Taunted; mocked (6)
The act of chasing after something (7)
Thin and bony (5)
To one side (5)
Unclear (10)
Worry (4)

Sounder Vocabulary Word Search 2

```
I N Q U I R I N G C U R I O S I T Y Y Z
S U F F O C A T E D P U N C T U A T E D
C Q P L A I N T I V E U J S D R S I N S
R P R N D X Y R Y C G Y R A T I O N S D
P D E S A C N E I F A M I S H E D D E R
R C C V M T L S D B K D S B U K W I S T
N O I K P A T M J J T K D Y W I R S H E
F M S R E E S A K G S R S L H A T T V R
D P I J R D E S U O L L A C E V E I R G
B U O N E N C H U Y C E Y W T D S N V L
K L N V G E X E J R Q H E D E S W C A R
R S N A A L R N H R E N D N E D Z T S Z
D I M C S S E E X A B D I C E F R V T M
L O P C K B G D D U D A C T R A I I T G
W N A I E P A T Q Q R U A E J T C A L G
G D R N W R U Q H T S T T A A K D S N V
L D C A W D N C S Z I H S L I V C V Q T
Q C H T Q F T N L S P Q S N D B N H T V
Q V E E C D O F E Y Y D G T A N N E R Y
H J D W F C L H V I S U A L I Z E D Q W
```

A receptacle for holding water, especially rain water (7)
Accuracy; exactness (9)
An adjustable plate in the flue of a furnace or stove for controlling the draft (6)
An irresistible motivation to do something (10)
Asking (9)
Body organs necessary for life (6)
Boldly resisting (7)
Confined; restrained; held back (11)
Confused (6)
Distress; cause to be sorrowful (6)
Enclosed (7)
Establishment where hides are tanned (7)
Extremely hungry (8)
Following in uninterrupted order; consecutive (10)
Formed a mental image (10)
Great in size; huge (4)
Hardened; toughened (9)
Interrupted periodically (10)
Joy (4)
Lacking brightness or clarity (3)
Made certain; guaranteed; made confident (7)
Made dry (7)
Mattress or pillow cover made of strong cotton (7)
Mixed (7)
Mournful; melancholy (9)
Movements (9)
Pale (5)
Partially opened (4)
Paused in uncertainty (9)
Physically or emotionally tired (7)
Prey; a hunted animal (6)
Sharpen (4)
Something that arouses interest (9)
Stifled (10)
Taunted; mocked (6)
The act of chasing after something (7)
Thin and bony (5)
To give a vaccine to produce an immunity to an infectious disease (9)
To one side (5)
Unclear (10)
Worry (4)

Sounder Vocabulary Word Search 2 Answer Key

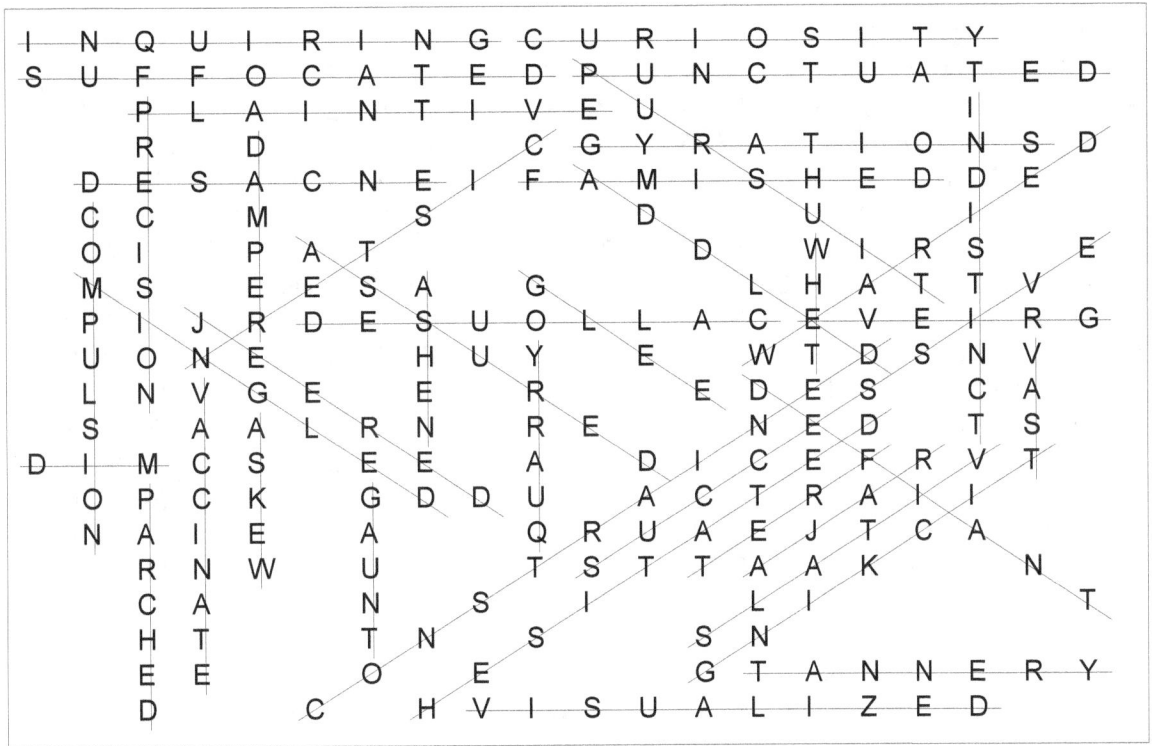

A receptacle for holding water, especially rain water (7)
Accuracy; exactness (9)
An adjustable plate in the flue of a furnace or stove for controlling the draft (6)
An irresistible motivation to do something (10)
Asking (9)
Body organs necessary for life (6)
Boldly resisting (7)
Confined; restrained; held back (11)
Confused (6)
Distress; cause to be sorrowful (6)
Enclosed (7)
Establishment where hides are tanned (7)
Extremely hungry (8)
Following in uninterrupted order; consecutive (10)
Formed a mental image (10)
Great in size; huge (4)
Hardened; toughened (9)
Interrupted periodically (10)
Joy (4)
Lacking brightness or clarity (3)

Made certain; guaranteed; made confident (7)
Made dry (7)
Mattress or pillow cover made of strong cotton (7)
Mixed (7)
Mournful; melancholy (9)
Movements (9)
Pale (5)
Partially opened (4)
Paused in uncertainty (9)
Physically or emotionally tired (7)
Prey; a hunted animal (6)
Sharpen (4)
Something that arouses interest (9)
Stifled (10)
Taunted; mocked (6)
The act of chasing after something (7)
Thin and bony (5)
To give a vaccine to produce an immunity to an infectious disease (9)
To one side (5)
Unclear (10)
Worry (4)

Sounder Vocabulary Word Search 3

```
P W V C O N S T R A I N E D P L A I N T I V E H P
R L N I O Z S G B C M L S M W D Q J R I F P G E L
E K G W S M Q U N K N C X H D E J L E C B X D S D
C T L S V U P X C W D C Y L T H C R T K M V E I C
I K Y C A K A U K C M L E W X S G S A I B D T T H
S D L R J K W L L N E D K S V I W S N N G Q A A X
I U R I N T B N I S H S T F F M F H I G D Y U T K
O Y N L N Q L F S Z I C S W K A W S C H S Y T E C
N W M C W Q S Y V S E O R I N F U T C P D V C D Y
L R R X E V U N K J K D N L V F G T A V B U N N M
D R K G A R Y I E C G X G X F E P Q V N R F U N F
E W P G R Q T E R W A K F O L M E V W I N N P C P
S M D A I W R A V I U P C T L S V H O D M E C Y X
U J L S E E C T I I N A U E W D E S G E T C R D D
O C T S D E F I A N T G Y R A T I O N S G J E Y W
L H N U S N S T S E T A N F S T R M A A F L M R X
L D H R P C F S D T B Y L G Y U G V R C G V E B N
A S H E N P A R C H E D J S B M I A Z N T X N E V
C M X D T M B Q R X P R S R Y M J T I E T Z K Z N
A S K E W I N D I S T I N C T A R M D A M P E R P
```

ADDLED	DEFIANT	INQUIRING	TANNERY
AJAR	DIM	JEERED	TICKING
ASHEN	ENCASED	MINGLED	UNCERTAINTY
ASKEW	FAMISHED	PARCHED	VACCINATE
ASSURED	FRET	PLAINTIVE	VAST
CALLOUSED	GAUNT	PRECISION	VISUALIZED
CISTERN	GLEE	PUNCTUATED	VITALS
COMPULSION	GRIEVE	PURSUIT	WEARIED
CONSTRAINED	GYRATIONS	QUARRY	WHET
CURIOSITY	HESITATED	SUCCESSIVE	
DAMPER	INDISTINCT	SUFFOCATED	

Sounder Vocabulary Word Search 3 Answer Key

ADDLED	DEFIANT	INQUIRING	TANNERY
AJAR	DIM	JEERED	TICKING
ASHEN	ENCASED	MINGLED	UNCERTAINTY
ASKEW	FAMISHED	PARCHED	VACCINATE
ASSURED	FRET	PLAINTIVE	VAST
CALLOUSED	GAUNT	PRECISION	VISUALIZED
CISTERN	GLEE	PUNCTUATED	VITALS
COMPULSION	GRIEVE	PURSUIT	WEARIED
CONSTRAINED	GYRATIONS	QUARRY	WHET
CURIOSITY	HESITATED	SUCCESSIVE	
DAMPER	INDISTINCT	SUFFOCATED	

Sounder Vocabulary Word Search 4

```
Q W V U N C E R T A I N T Y M P T F K B B F B Q W
S C I P W W Y Q F I W C T G V A C C I N A T E Q J
Z M S D B D L Q Z R N S N S M H N K N X J P P L C
G C U H E G T Z W F X Q M L E D I W G S Q S P B F
V M A Z T F D X N G T R U S W X T B P G Q K W P X
J C L B X A I X V A J F I I N V S V J Z D E Q P K
G G I Y M D W A C U R T B M R C I A M K K M D F H
P L Z P H E V J N N A P D I V I D S Z S I J T H F
U D E H S I M A F T D E L D D A N T A N N E R Y Z
N R D E T R C M E E R D E A S O I G G M R E R K H
C B S A B A P D H U E T H H I X W L V F G R S V S
T F L Q R E F C S N A T E S E N E H C M A E U J T
U S G P T W R S I C I N I V P D T C E U P D C I L
A J L Z B A A A O U C C E D C F J I Q T G M C E V
T K L W P V R F S W E I P A W S J H V Q K K E N T
E V Q P T T F R H R R B S N J C F C N E I L S C X
D K B M S U U H P G C W F T L A Z K B N C F S A C
H G Y N S P F G T K G C X H E F R J G W B W I S D
T H O C A L L O U S E D P G Y R A T I O N S V E X
H C K L K C U R I O S I T Y S K N F D G X P E D T
```

ADDLED	DIM	JEERED	TICKING
AJAR	ENCASED	MINGLED	UNCERTAINTY
ASHEN	FAMISHED	PARCHED	VACCINATE
ASKEW	FRET	PLAINTIVE	VAST
ASSURED	GAUNT	PRECISION	VISUALIZED
CALLOUSED	GLEE	PUNCTUATED	VITALS
CISTERN	GRIEVE	PURSUIT	WEARIED
CONSTRAINED	GYRATIONS	QUARRY	WHET
CURIOSITY	HESITATED	SUCCESSIVE	
DAMPER	INDISTINCT	SUFFOCATED	
DEFIANT	INQUIRING	TANNERY	

Sounder Vocabulary Word Search 4 Answer Key

ADDLED	DIM	JEERED	TICKING
AJAR	ENCASED	MINGLED	UNCERTAINTY
ASHEN	FAMISHED	PARCHED	VACCINATE
ASKEW	FRET	PLAINTIVE	VAST
ASSURED	GAUNT	PRECISION	VISUALIZED
CALLOUSED	GLEE	PUNCTUATED	VITALS
CISTERN	GRIEVE	PURSUIT	WEARIED
CONSTRAINED	GYRATIONS	QUARRY	WHET
CURIOSITY	HESITATED	SUCCESSIVE	
DAMPER	INDISTINCT	SUFFOCATED	
DEFIANT	INQUIRING	TANNERY	

Sounder Vocabulary Crossword 1

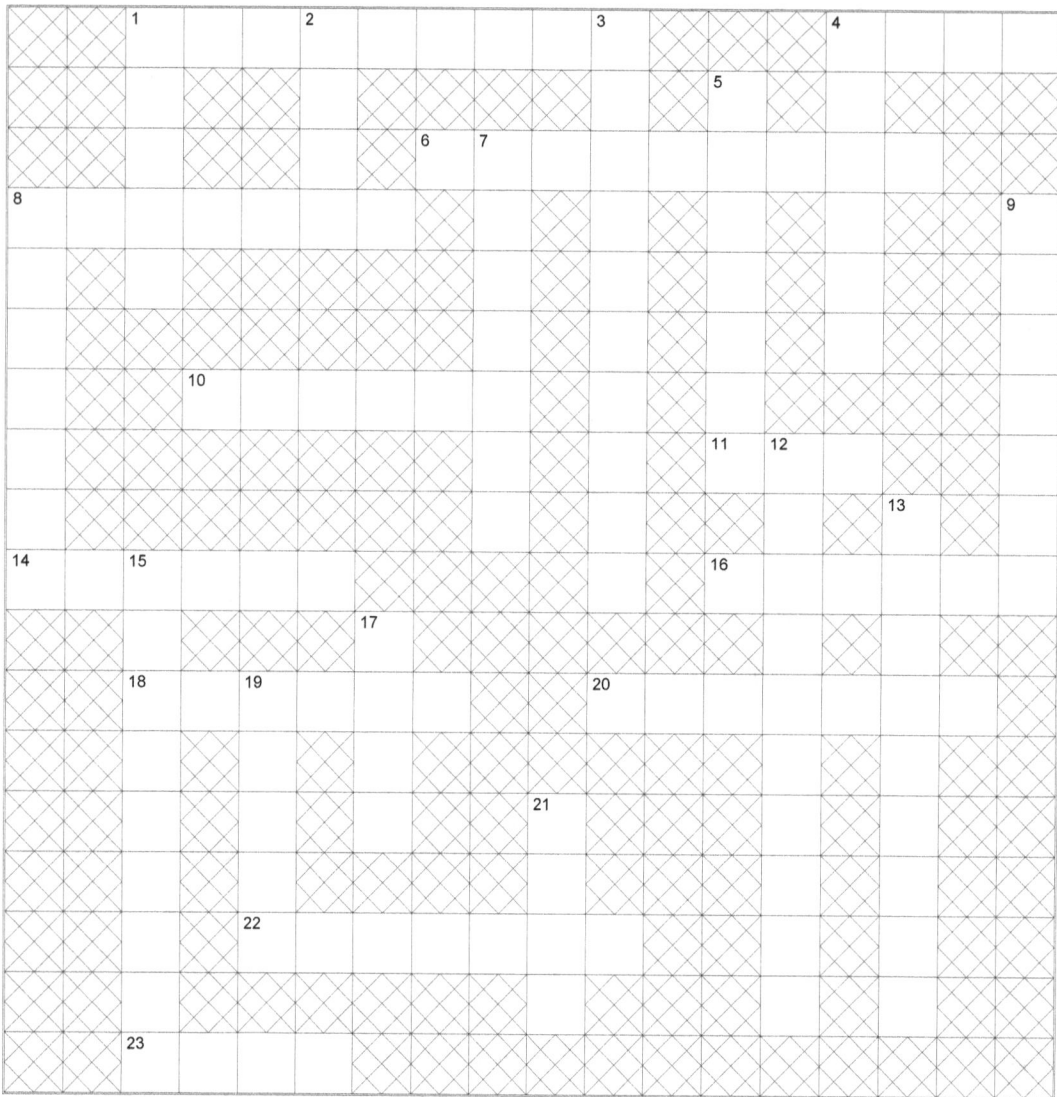

Across
1. Movements
4. Great in size; huge
6. To give a vaccine to produce an immunity to an infectious disease
8. Establishment where hides are tanned
10. An adjustable plate in the flue of a furnace or stove for controlling the draft
11. Lacking brightness or clarity
14. Distress; cause to be sorrowful
16. Confused
18. Prey; a hunted animal
20. The act of chasing after something
22. Physically or emotionally tired
23. Joy

Down
1. Thin and bony
2. Partially opened
3. Following in uninterrupted order; consecutive
4. Body organs necessary for life
5. Enclosed
7. Made certain; guaranteed; made confident
8. Mattress or pillow cover made of strong cotton
9. Made dry
12. Unclear
13. Mournful; melancholy
15. Asking
17. Worry
19. To one side
21. Sharpen

Sounder Vocabulary Crossword 1 Answer Key

		1 G	Y	R	2 A	T	I	O	N	3 S			4 V	A	S	T
		A			J					U		5 E	I			
		U			A		6 V	7 A	C	C	I	N	A	T	E	
8 T	A	N	N	E	R	Y		S		C		C		A		9 P
I		T						S		E		A		L		A
C								U		S		S		S		R
K			10 D	A	M	P	E	R		S		E				C
I								E		I		11 D	12 I	M		H
N								D		V		I		13 P		E
14 G	R	15 I	E	V	E					E		16 A	D	D	L	E	D
		N			17 F								I		A		
		18 Q	U	19 A	R	R	Y			20 P	U	R	S	U	I	T
		U		S		E					T		N			
		I		K		T		21 W					I		T	
		R		E				H					N		I	
		I		22 W	E	A	R	I	E	D			C		V	
		N						T					T		E	
		23 G	L	E	E											

Across
1. Movements
4. Great in size; huge
6. To give a vaccine to produce an immunity to an infectious disease
8. Establishment where hides are tanned
10. An adjustable plate in the flue of a furnace or stove for controlling the draft
11. Lacking brightness or clarity
14. Distress; cause to be sorrowful
16. Confused
18. Prey; a hunted animal
20. The act of chasing after something
22. Physically or emotionally tired
23. Joy

Down
1. Thin and bony
2. Partially opened
3. Following in uninterrupted order; consecutive
4. Body organs necessary for life
5. Enclosed
7. Made certain; guaranteed; made confident
8. Mattress or pillow cover made of strong cotton
9. Made dry
12. Unclear
13. Mournful; melancholy
15. Asking
17. Worry
19. To one side
21. Sharpen

Sounder Vocabulary Crossword 2

Across
2. An adjustable plate in the flue of a furnace or stove for controlling the draft
5. Joy
6. Body organs necessary for life
7. Distress; cause to be sorrowful
9. Partially opened
10. Thin and bony
12. Mattress or pillow cover made of strong cotton
16. Made certain; guaranteed; made confident
17. Sharpen
21. Lacking brightness or clarity
22. Taunted; mocked
23. Worry

Down
1. Physically or emotionally tired
2. Boldly resisting
3. Mixed
4. Pale
5. Movements
8. Great in size; huge
9. Confused
11. To one side
13. Unclear
14. Hardened; toughened
15. Following in uninterrupted order; consecutive
18. Paused in uncertainty
19. Establishment where hides are tanned
20. A receptacle for holding water, especially rain water

Sounder Vocabulary Crossword 2 Answer Key

Across
2. An adjustable plate in the flue of a furnace or stove for controlling the draft
5. Joy
6. Body organs necessary for life
7. Distress; cause to be sorrowful
9. Partially opened
10. Thin and bony
12. Mattress or pillow cover made of strong cotton
16. Made certain; guaranteed; made confident
17. Sharpen
21. Lacking brightness or clarity
22. Taunted; mocked
23. Worry

Down
1. Physically or emotionally tired
2. Boldly resisting
3. Mixed
4. Pale
5. Movements
8. Great in size; huge
9. Confused
11. To one side
13. Unclear
14. Hardened; toughened
15. Following in uninterrupted order; consecutive
18. Paused in uncertainty
19. Establishment where hides are tanned
20. A receptacle for holding water, especially rain water

Sounder Vocabulary Crossword 3

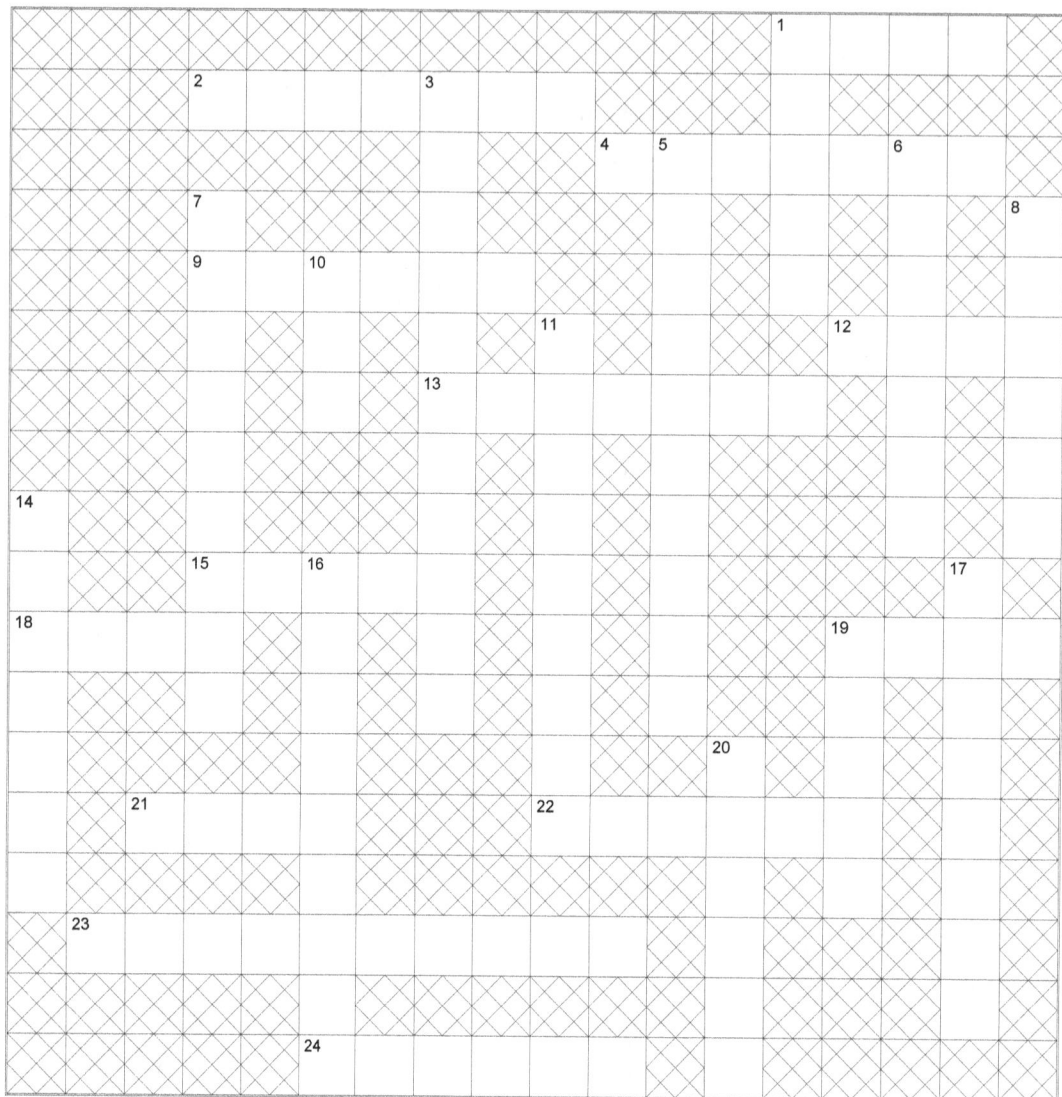

Across
1. Joy
2. The act of chasing after something
4. Made certain; guaranteed; made confident
9. Confused
12. Great in size; huge
13. Establishment where hides are tanned
15. Pale
18. Worry
19. Partially opened
21. Sharpen
22. Distress; cause to be sorrowful
23. Interrupted periodically
24. An adjustable plate in the flue of a furnace or stove for controlling the draft

Down
1. Thin and bony
3. Doubtfulness; not knowing for sure
5. Following in uninterrupted order; consecutive
6. Enclosed
7. To give a vaccine to produce an immunity to an infectious disease
8. Body organs necessary for life
10. Lacking brightness or clarity
11. Asking
14. Boldly resisting
16. Paused in uncertainty
17. Extremely hungry
19. To one side
20. Taunted; mocked

Sounder Vocabulary Crossword 3 Answer Key

Across
1. Joy
2. The act of chasing after something
4. Made certain; guaranteed; made confident
9. Confused
12. Great in size; huge
13. Establishment where hides are tanned
15. Pale
18. Worry
19. Partially opened
21. Sharpen
22. Distress; cause to be sorrowful
23. Interrupted periodically
24. An adjustable plate in the flue of a furnace or stove for controlling the draft

Down
1. Thin and bony
3. Doubtfulness; not knowing for sure
5. Following in uninterrupted order; consecutive
6. Enclosed
7. To give a vaccine to produce an immunity to an infectious disease
8. Body organs necessary for life
10. Lacking brightness or clarity
11. Asking
14. Boldly resisting
16. Paused in uncertainty
17. Extremely hungry
19. To one side
20. Taunted; mocked

Sounder Vocabulary Crossword 4

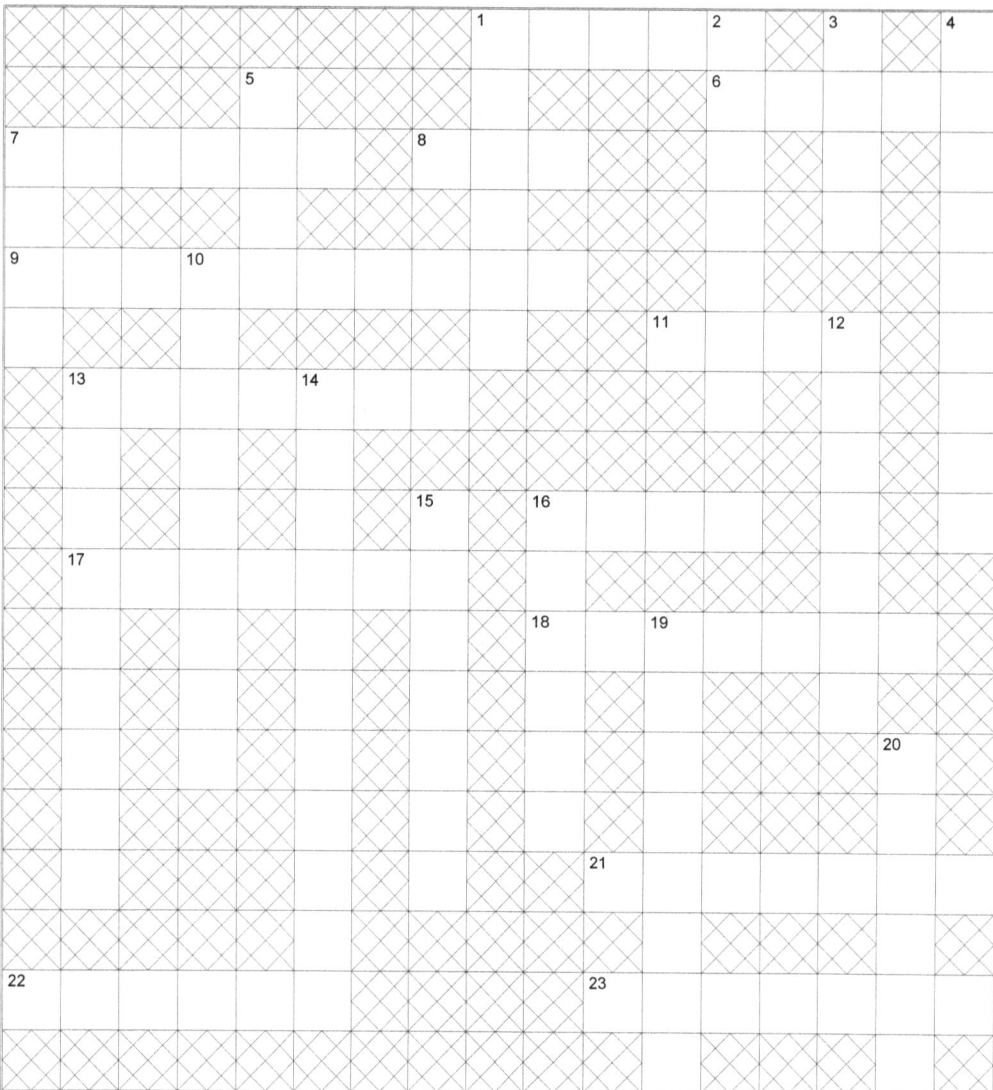

Across
1. Thin and bony
6. Pale
7. Body organs necessary for life
8. Lacking brightness or clarity
9. Following in uninterrupted order; consecutive
11. Worry
13. The act of chasing after something
16. Partially opened
17. A receptacle for holding water, especially rain water
18. Boldly resisting
21. Made certain; guaranteed; made confident
22. Prey; a hunted animal
23. Physically or emotionally tired

Down
1. Distress; cause to be sorrowful
2. Establishment where hides are tanned
3. Sharpen
4. Asking
5. Joy
7. Great in size; huge
10. Something that arouses interest
12. Mattress or pillow cover made of strong cotton
13. Accuracy; exactness
14. Doubtfulness; not knowing for sure
15. Enclosed
16. Confused
19. Extremely hungry
20. Taunted; mocked

Sounder Vocabulary Crossword 4 Answer Key

Across
1. Thin and bony
6. Pale
7. Body organs necessary for life
8. Lacking brightness or clarity
9. Following in uninterrupted order; consecutive
11. Worry
13. The act of chasing after something
16. Partially opened
17. A receptacle for holding water, especially rain water
18. Boldly resisting
21. Made certain; guaranteed; made confident
22. Prey; a hunted animal
23. Physically or emotionally tired

Down
1. Distress; cause to be sorrowful
2. Establishment where hides are tanned
3. Sharpen
4. Asking
5. Joy
7. Great in size; huge
10. Something that arouses interest
12. Mattress or pillow cover made of strong cotton
13. Accuracy; exactness
14. Doubtfulness; not knowing for sure
15. Enclosed
16. Confused
19. Extremely hungry
20. Taunted; mocked

Sounder Vocabulary Juggle Letters 1

1. TREF = 1. _____
   Worry

2. ENYRNTA = 2. _____
   Establishment where hides are tanned

3. ORICSIPEN = 3. _____
   Accuracy; exactness

4. ENDTSRINCOA = 4. _____
   Confined; restrained; held back

5. PMRADE = 5. _____
   An adjustable plate in the flue of a furnace or stove for controlling the draft

6. UNAGT = 6. _____
   Thin and bony

7. IEETAHDTS = 7. _____
   Paused in uncertainty

8. EIDTANF = 8. _____
   Boldly resisting

9. EDADDL = 9. _____
   Confused

10. TEHW =10. _____
    Sharpen

11. SATV =11. _____
    Great in size; huge

12. ADSEIMFH =12. _____
    Extremely hungry

13. GLIMEND =13. _____
    Mixed

14. RATNOGISY =14. _____
    Movements

15. OMUCIOSLNP =15. _____
    An irresistible motivation to do something

Sounder Vocabulary Juggle Letters 1 Answer Key

1. TREF = 1. FRET
   Worry

2. ENYRNTA = 2. TANNERY
   Establishment where hides are tanned

3. ORICSIPEN = 3. PRECISION
   Accuracy; exactness

4. ENDTSRINCOA = 4. CONSTRAINED
   Confined; restrained; held back

5. PMRADE = 5. DAMPER
   An adjustable plate in the flue of a furnace or stove for controlling the draft

6. UNAGT = 6. GAUNT
   Thin and bony

7. IEETAHDTS = 7. HESITATED
   Paused in uncertainty

8. EIDTANF = 8. DEFIANT
   Boldly resisting

9. EDADDL = 9. ADDLED
   Confused

10. TEHW = 10. WHET
    Sharpen

11. SATV = 11. VAST
    Great in size; huge

12. ADSEIMFH = 12. FAMISHED
    Extremely hungry

13. GLIMEND = 13. MINGLED
    Mixed

14. RATNOGISY = 14. GYRATIONS
    Movements

15. OMUCIOSLNP = 15. COMPULSION
    An irresistible motivation to do something

Sounder Vocabulary Juggle Letters 2

1. UCAOFFTDSE = 1. _____
   Stifled

2. SICIORNPE = 2. _____
   Accuracy; exactness

3. TAUNUPCTDE = 3. _____
   Interrupted periodically

4. UIUTSRP = 4. _____
   The act of chasing after something

5. GNMIEDL = 5. _____
   Mixed

6. NCIREST = 6. _____
   A receptacle for holding water, especially rain water

7. ADFITNE = 7. _____
   Boldly resisting

8. EGIEVR = 8. _____
   Distress; cause to be sorrowful

9. LGEE = 9. _____
   Joy

10. SESAUDR =10. _____
    Made certain; guaranteed; made confident

11. JARA =11. _____
    Partially opened

12. DADLED =12. _____
    Confused

13. ASIVEZUDIL =13. _____
    Formed a mental image

14. TYGINSORA =14. _____
    Movements

15. USNOIOCLMP =15. _____
    An irresistible motivation to do something

Sounder Vocabulary Juggle Letters 2 Answer Key

1. UCAOFFTDSE = 1. SUFFOCATED
   Stifled

2. SICIORNPE = 2. PRECISION
   Accuracy; exactness

3. TAUNUPCTDE = 3. PUNCTUATED
   Interrupted periodically

4. UIUTSRP = 4. PURSUIT
   The act of chasing after something

5. GNMIEDL = 5. MINGLED
   Mixed

6. NCIREST = 6. CISTERN
   A receptacle for holding water, especially rain water

7. ADFITNE = 7. DEFIANT
   Boldly resisting

8. EGIEVR = 8. GRIEVE
   Distress; cause to be sorrowful

9. LGEE = 9. GLEE
   Joy

10. SESAUDR =10. ASSURED
    Made certain; guaranteed; made confident

11. JARA =11. AJAR
    Partially opened

12. DADLED =12. ADDLED
    Confused

13. ASIVEZUDIL =13. VISUALIZED
    Formed a mental image

14. TYGINSORA =14. GYRATIONS
    Movements

15. USNOIOCLMP =15. COMPULSION
    An irresistible motivation to do something

Sounder Vocabulary Juggle Letters 3

1. SCPIIENOR = 1. _____
   Accuracy; exactness

2. CECNVATAI = 2. _____
   To give a vaccine to produce an immunity to an infectious disease

3. LONIOCUSMP = 3. _____
   An irresistible motivation to do something

4. JRAA = 4. _____
   Partially opened

5. EERGIV = 5. _____
   Distress; cause to be sorrowful

6. RASIYGNTO = 6. _____
   Movements

7. TININSTICD = 7. _____
   Unclear

8. TITCUANNEYR = 8. _____
   Doubtfulness; not knowing for sure

9. ERJEDE = 9. _____
   Taunted; mocked

10. IDSCNEROANT =10. _____
    Confined; restrained; held back

11. OUISRCTIY =11. _____
    Something that arouses interest

12. AEPITLVIN =12. _____
    Mournful; melancholy

13. GUNTA =13. _____
    Thin and bony

14. MASEFIDH =14. _____
    Extremely hungry

15. ESDCEAN =15. _____
    Enclosed

Sounder Vocabulary Juggle Letters 3 Answer Key

1. SCPIIENOR = 1. PRECISION
Accuracy; exactness

2. CECNVATAI = 2. VACCINATE
To give a vaccine to produce an immunity to an infectious disease

3. LONIOCUSMP = 3. COMPULSION
An irresistible motivation to do something

4. JRAA = 4. AJAR
Partially opened

5. EERGIV = 5. GRIEVE
Distress; cause to be sorrowful

6. RASIYGNTO = 6. GYRATIONS
Movements

7. TININSTICD = 7. INDISTINCT
Unclear

8. TITCUANNEYR = 8. UNCERTAINTY
Doubtfulness; not knowing for sure

9. ERJEDE = 9. JEERED
Taunted; mocked

10. IDSCNEROANT = 10. CONSTRAINED
Confined; restrained; held back

11. OUISRCTIY = 11. CURIOSITY
Something that arouses interest

12. AEPITLVIN = 12. PLAINTIVE
Mournful; melancholy

13. GUNTA = 13. GAUNT
Thin and bony

14. MASEFIDH = 14. FAMISHED
Extremely hungry

15. ESDCEAN = 15. ENCASED
Enclosed

Sounder Vocabulary Juggle Letters 4

1. ARYUQR = 1. _____
Prey; a hunted animal

2. ELAUCSOLD = 2. _____
Hardened; toughened

3. ITNCGIK = 3. _____
Mattress or pillow cover made of strong cotton

4. EILNGDM = 4. _____
Mixed

5. NCIRSET = 5. _____
A receptacle for holding water, especially rain water

6. NOLSIOCPUM = 6. _____
An irresistible motivation to do something

7. NERTAYN = 7. _____
Establishment where hides are tanned

8. UAGTN = 8. _____
Thin and bony

9. CECNIAVAT = 9. _____
To give a vaccine to produce an immunity to an infectious disease

10. SIUSVCESEC =10. _____
Following in uninterrupted order; consecutive

11. URUSPTI =11. _____
The act of chasing after something

12. ITIEVLANP =12. _____
Mournful; melancholy

13. ETWH =13. _____
Sharpen

14. TUDANCUPET =14. _____
Interrupted periodically

15. EVIGER =15. _____
Distress; cause to be sorrowful

Sounder Vocabulary Juggle Letters 4 Answer Key

1. ARYUQR = 1. QUARRY
   Prey; a hunted animal

2. ELAUCSOLD = 2. CALLOUSED
   Hardened; toughened

3. ITNCGIK = 3. TICKING
   Mattress or pillow cover made of strong cotton

4. EILNGDM = 4. MINGLED
   Mixed

5. NCIRSET = 5. CISTERN
   A receptacle for holding water, especially rain water

6. NOLSIOCPUM = 6. COMPULSION
   An irresistible motivation to do something

7. NERTAYN = 7. TANNERY
   Establishment where hides are tanned

8. UAGTN = 8. GAUNT
   Thin and bony

9. CECNIAVAT = 9. VACCINATE
   To give a vaccine to produce an immunity to an infectious disease

10. SIUSVCESEC =10. SUCCESSIVE
    Following in uninterrupted order; consecutive

11. URUSPTI =11. PURSUIT
    The act of chasing after something

12. ITIEVLANP =12. PLAINTIVE
    Mournful; melancholy

13. ETWH =13. WHET
    Sharpen

14. TUDANCUPET =14. PUNCTUATED
    Interrupted periodically

15. EVIGER =15. GRIEVE
    Distress; cause to be sorrowful

ADDLED	Confused
AJAR	Partially opened
ASHEN	Pale
ASKEW	To one side
ASSURED	Made certain; guaranteed; made confident
CALLOUSED	Hardened; toughened

CISTERN	A receptacle for holding water, especially rain water
COMPULSION	An irresistible motivation to do something
CONSTRAINED	Confined; restrained; held back
CURIOSITY	Something that arouses interest
DAMPER	An adjustable plate in the flue of a furnace or stove for controlling the draft
DEFIANT	Boldly resisting

DIM	Lacking brightness or clarity
ENCASED	Enclosed
FAMISHED	Extremely hungry
FRET	Worry
GAUNT	Thin and bony
GLEE	Joy

GRIEVE	Distress; cause to be sorrowful
GYRATIONS	Movements
HESITATED	Paused in uncertainty
INDISTINCT	Unclear
INQUIRING	Asking
JEERED	Taunted; mocked

MINGLED	Mixed
PARCHED	Made dry
PLAINTIVE	Mournful; melancholy
PRECISION	Accuracy; exactness
PUNCTUATED	Interrupted periodically
PURSUIT	The act of chasing after something

QUARRY	Prey; a hunted animal
SUCCESSIVE	Following in uninterrupted order; consecutive
SUFFOCATED	Stifled
TANNERY	Establishment where hides are tanned
TICKING	Mattress or pillow cover made of strong cotton
UNCERTAINTY	Doubtfulness; not knowing for sure

VACCINATE	To give a vaccine to produce an immunity to an infectious disease
VAST	Great in size; huge
VISUALIZED	Formed a mental image
VITALS	Body organs necessary for life
WEARIED	Physically or emotionally tired
WHET	Sharpen

Sounder Vocabulary

VITALS	GLEE	ASSURED	GAUNT	PURSUIT
AJAR	TICKING	QUARRY	JEERED	WHET
INQUIRING	GYRATIONS	FREE SPACE	SUFFOCATED	CALLOUSED
HESITATED	PARCHED	CURIOSITY	CONSTRAINED	UNCERTAINTY
GRIEVE	VAST	PLAINTIVE	COMPULSION	ASHEN

Sounder Vocabulary

PRECISION	DEFIANT	INDISTINCT	WEARIED	TANNERY
ENCASED	CISTERN	DIM	FRET	VACCINATE
PUNCTUATED	VISUALIZED	FREE SPACE	ADDLED	ASKEW
MINGLED	FAMISHED	ASHEN	COMPULSION	PLAINTIVE
VAST	GRIEVE	UNCERTAINTY	CONSTRAINED	CURIOSITY

Sounder Vocabulary

GLEE	WEARIED	PLAINTIVE	UNCERTAINTY	MINGLED
VITALS	CALLOUSED	VACCINATE	VISUALIZED	ASHEN
FRET	ASKEW	FREE SPACE	TANNERY	CISTERN
COMPULSION	JEERED	QUARRY	WHET	FAMISHED
DEFIANT	CURIOSITY	SUCCESSIVE	ASSURED	CONSTRAINED

Sounder Vocabulary

TICKING	PURSUIT	GYRATIONS	SUFFOCATED	INQUIRING
PARCHED	DIM	DAMPER	AJAR	PRECISION
ADDLED	GRIEVE	FREE SPACE	ENCASED	GAUNT
HESITATED	VAST	CONSTRAINED	ASSURED	SUCCESSIVE
CURIOSITY	DEFIANT	FAMISHED	WHET	QUARRY

Sounder Vocabulary

FRET	DIM	VACCINATE	PUNCTUATED	ADDLED
INDISTINCT	WHET	QUARRY	HESITATED	GYRATIONS
GAUNT	PARCHED	FREE SPACE	PLAINTIVE	DAMPER
FAMISHED	TANNERY	CURIOSITY	GLEE	JEERED
CONSTRAINED	VAST	INQUIRING	VISUALIZED	COMPULSION

Sounder Vocabulary

ASSURED	ASHEN	PURSUIT	ASKEW	WEARIED
UNCERTAINTY	DEFIANT	ENCASED	CISTERN	GRIEVE
SUCCESSIVE	CALLOUSED	FREE SPACE	SUFFOCATED	PRECISION
TICKING	VITALS	COMPULSION	VISUALIZED	INQUIRING
VAST	CONSTRAINED	JEERED	GLEE	CURIOSITY

Sounder Vocabulary

COMPULSION	INDISTINCT	GRIEVE	ASSURED	MINGLED
INQUIRING	TICKING	ASKEW	JEERED	FRET
DIM	CONSTRAINED	FREE SPACE	ENCASED	PURSUIT
HESITATED	VACCINATE	GAUNT	VISUALIZED	GYRATIONS
WHET	QUARRY	PARCHED	ADDLED	CALLOUSED

Sounder Vocabulary

DEFIANT	PRECISION	WEARIED	PLAINTIVE	CURIOSITY
VITALS	DAMPER	AJAR	ASHEN	VAST
PUNCTUATED	SUFFOCATED	FREE SPACE	SUCCESSIVE	TANNERY
FAMISHED	GLEE	CALLOUSED	ADDLED	PARCHED
QUARRY	WHET	GYRATIONS	VISUALIZED	GAUNT

Sounder Vocabulary

AJAR	WEARIED	GLEE	WHET	GRIEVE
JEERED	ASKEW	MINGLED	ADDLED	TANNERY
CISTERN	CONSTRAINED	FREE SPACE	PARCHED	HESITATED
CALLOUSED	SUFFOCATED	INQUIRING	VAST	UNCERTAINTY
DAMPER	ASSURED	COMPULSION	PUNCTUATED	VITALS

Sounder Vocabulary

PURSUIT	ASHEN	GYRATIONS	FAMISHED	TICKING
INDISTINCT	VACCINATE	FRET	PLAINTIVE	QUARRY
CURIOSITY	PRECISION	FREE SPACE	VISUALIZED	SUCCESSIVE
DIM	ENCASED	VITALS	PUNCTUATED	COMPULSION
ASSURED	DAMPER	UNCERTAINTY	VAST	INQUIRING

Sounder Vocabulary

GLEE	SUCCESSIVE	VITALS	PUNCTUATED	INDISTINCT
TICKING	HESITATED	VAST	WHET	DIM
ADDLED	CONSTRAINED	FREE SPACE	ASHEN	PLAINTIVE
PARCHED	GAUNT	PURSUIT	JEERED	UNCERTAINTY
WEARIED	DAMPER	SUFFOCATED	CURIOSITY	QUARRY

Sounder Vocabulary

MINGLED	COMPULSION	TANNERY	ASSURED	DEFIANT
VACCINATE	ASKEW	CALLOUSED	FAMISHED	INQUIRING
PRECISION	GYRATIONS	FREE SPACE	AJAR	CISTERN
FRET	ENCASED	QUARRY	CURIOSITY	SUFFOCATED
DAMPER	WEARIED	UNCERTAINTY	JEERED	PURSUIT

Sounder Vocabulary

GLEE	ADDLED	VITALS	AJAR	SUFFOCATED
GAUNT	PRECISION	PLAINTIVE	VACCINATE	UNCERTAINTY
SUCCESSIVE	MINGLED	FREE SPACE	WEARIED	ENCASED
JEERED	VISUALIZED	ASHEN	PUNCTUATED	CISTERN
DAMPER	PARCHED	CALLOUSED	GYRATIONS	HESITATED

Sounder Vocabulary

TICKING	CONSTRAINED	DIM	WHET	COMPULSION
TANNERY	DEFIANT	INQUIRING	ASSURED	ASKEW
FRET	INDISTINCT	FREE SPACE	VAST	PURSUIT
GRIEVE	CURIOSITY	HESITATED	GYRATIONS	CALLOUSED
PARCHED	DAMPER	CISTERN	PUNCTUATED	ASHEN

Sounder Vocabulary

COMPULSION	ENCASED	INQUIRING	FRET	ASSURED
VAST	PARCHED	PURSUIT	AJAR	PLAINTIVE
GLEE	VISUALIZED	FREE SPACE	GYRATIONS	PUNCTUATED
DEFIANT	INDISTINCT	UNCERTAINTY	FAMISHED	CONSTRAINED
CISTERN	WHET	JEERED	SUCCESSIVE	CALLOUSED

Sounder Vocabulary

TICKING	SUFFOCATED	QUARRY	WEARIED	MINGLED
PRECISION	DAMPER	VITALS	HESITATED	DIM
GRIEVE	CURIOSITY	FREE SPACE	VACCINATE	ADDLED
TANNERY	GAUNT	CALLOUSED	SUCCESSIVE	JEERED
WHET	CISTERN	CONSTRAINED	FAMISHED	UNCERTAINTY

Sounder Vocabulary

WEARIED	PURSUIT	FAMISHED	COMPULSION	CONSTRAINED
DAMPER	MINGLED	PUNCTUATED	CURIOSITY	AJAR
SUCCESSIVE	VISUALIZED	FREE SPACE	TICKING	VACCINATE
PLAINTIVE	ASSURED	QUARRY	HESITATED	INDISTINCT
WHET	GYRATIONS	ASHEN	GAUNT	ENCASED

Sounder Vocabulary

CISTERN	DIM	PRECISION	ADDLED	ASKEW
VITALS	TANNERY	CALLOUSED	VAST	INQUIRING
DEFIANT	PARCHED	FREE SPACE	UNCERTAINTY	JEERED
GLEE	SUFFOCATED	ENCASED	GAUNT	ASHEN
GYRATIONS	WHET	INDISTINCT	HESITATED	QUARRY

Sounder Vocabulary

GRIEVE	ADDLED	INDISTINCT	CISTERN	PLAINTIVE
INQUIRING	PURSUIT	AJAR	TANNERY	GAUNT
PUNCTUATED	VISUALIZED	FREE SPACE	SUFFOCATED	PARCHED
DIM	PRECISION	CURIOSITY	WEARIED	CONSTRAINED
HESITATED	ENCASED	VACCINATE	MINGLED	FAMISHED

Sounder Vocabulary

QUARRY	TICKING	SUCCESSIVE	ASHEN	VAST
COMPULSION	FRET	WHET	GLEE	JEERED
CALLOUSED	GYRATIONS	FREE SPACE	DAMPER	UNCERTAINTY
ASKEW	DEFIANT	FAMISHED	MINGLED	VACCINATE
ENCASED	HESITATED	CONSTRAINED	WEARIED	CURIOSITY

Sounder Vocabulary

ADDLED	GRIEVE	VISUALIZED	VITALS	TICKING
VACCINATE	QUARRY	INQUIRING	SUCCESSIVE	DAMPER
FRET	CURIOSITY	FREE SPACE	DEFIANT	ASKEW
WHET	DIM	PRECISION	GYRATIONS	PUNCTUATED
FAMISHED	ASSURED	MINGLED	PARCHED	PLAINTIVE

Sounder Vocabulary

ENCASED	SUFFOCATED	VAST	WEARIED	HESITATED
INDISTINCT	UNCERTAINTY	GLEE	JEERED	PURSUIT
ASHEN	CALLOUSED	FREE SPACE	CISTERN	AJAR
COMPULSION	CONSTRAINED	PLAINTIVE	PARCHED	MINGLED
ASSURED	FAMISHED	PUNCTUATED	GYRATIONS	PRECISION

Sounder Vocabulary

PRECISION	COMPULSION	INQUIRING	GLEE	PUNCTUATED
PLAINTIVE	WEARIED	DEFIANT	ASKEW	ADDLED
ASHEN	DIM	FREE SPACE	GRIEVE	DAMPER
HESITATED	CALLOUSED	VACCINATE	MINGLED	PARCHED
INDISTINCT	CURIOSITY	VAST	TANNERY	GAUNT

Sounder Vocabulary

GYRATIONS	WHET	CISTERN	CONSTRAINED	FRET
TICKING	VITALS	SUFFOCATED	ASSURED	UNCERTAINTY
JEERED	SUCCESSIVE	FREE SPACE	PURSUIT	ENCASED
AJAR	FAMISHED	GAUNT	TANNERY	VAST
CURIOSITY	INDISTINCT	PARCHED	MINGLED	VACCINATE

Sounder Vocabulary

VAST	VITALS	GAUNT	WEARIED	PRECISION
GLEE	GYRATIONS	COMPULSION	ENCASED	FAMISHED
ASHEN	WHET	FREE SPACE	AJAR	INQUIRING
INDISTINCT	TANNERY	CONSTRAINED	HESITATED	CISTERN
DIM	UNCERTAINTY	ASSURED	GRIEVE	ADDLED

Sounder Vocabulary

SUFFOCATED	PUNCTUATED	PLAINTIVE	TICKING	QUARRY
MINGLED	PARCHED	SUCCESSIVE	ASKEW	VACCINATE
PURSUIT	VISUALIZED	FREE SPACE	FRET	CALLOUSED
DAMPER	CURIOSITY	ADDLED	GRIEVE	ASSURED
UNCERTAINTY	DIM	CISTERN	HESITATED	CONSTRAINED

Sounder Vocabulary

ENCASED	CONSTRAINED	GAUNT	DAMPER	UNCERTAINTY
GRIEVE	VISUALIZED	PRECISION	VACCINATE	HESITATED
ASKEW	FAMISHED	FREE SPACE	INDISTINCT	ASSURED
PUNCTUATED	CISTERN	COMPULSION	CURIOSITY	QUARRY
INQUIRING	GLEE	VAST	ADDLED	ASHEN

Sounder Vocabulary

FRET	TICKING	GYRATIONS	PLAINTIVE	DIM
SUCCESSIVE	VITALS	JEERED	SUFFOCATED	CALLOUSED
MINGLED	DEFIANT	FREE SPACE	TANNERY	AJAR
PURSUIT	WHET	ASHEN	ADDLED	VAST
GLEE	INQUIRING	QUARRY	CURIOSITY	COMPULSION

Sounder Vocabulary

AJAR	CALLOUSED	ASSURED	GRIEVE	TANNERY
MINGLED	DEFIANT	SUCCESSIVE	ASKEW	COMPULSION
DIM	GYRATIONS	FREE SPACE	PUNCTUATED	DAMPER
GLEE	PRECISION	PARCHED	ENCASED	VISUALIZED
UNCERTAINTY	CONSTRAINED	VACCINATE	HESITATED	QUARRY

Sounder Vocabulary

CISTERN	JEERED	TICKING	ADDLED	GAUNT
FRET	SUFFOCATED	WEARIED	VAST	INDISTINCT
INQUIRING	CURIOSITY	FREE SPACE	PLAINTIVE	FAMISHED
WHET	PURSUIT	QUARRY	HESITATED	VACCINATE
CONSTRAINED	UNCERTAINTY	VISUALIZED	ENCASED	PARCHED

Sounder Vocabulary

ADDLED	CONSTRAINED	WEARIED	QUARRY	COMPULSION
WHET	SUFFOCATED	SUCCESSIVE	VITALS	PUNCTUATED
CALLOUSED	VAST	FREE SPACE	PURSUIT	DIM
FRET	CISTERN	VACCINATE	DEFIANT	FAMISHED
GRIEVE	INQUIRING	AJAR	TICKING	UNCERTAINTY

Sounder Vocabulary

DAMPER	GYRATIONS	MINGLED	GLEE	ENCASED
VISUALIZED	ASKEW	ASHEN	PRECISION	ASSURED
HESITATED	TANNERY	FREE SPACE	JEERED	PLAINTIVE
PARCHED	CURIOSITY	UNCERTAINTY	TICKING	AJAR
INQUIRING	GRIEVE	FAMISHED	DEFIANT	VACCINATE

www.ingramcontent.com/pod-product-compliance
Lightning Source LLC
Chambersburg PA
CBHW081457070526
44586CB00019B/2396